*What is your position regarding
the race crisis?*

*What should the Christian church do
when the community changes?*

Isn't the Negro

basically religious?

*Won't integration lead to intermarriage
and mongrelization of the races?*

BLACK AND FREE

The Skinners

BLACK AND FREE

TOM SKINNER

ZONDERVAN PUBLISHING HOUSE
Grand Rapids, Michigan

Special edition published for
TOM SKINNER CRUSADES, INC.
521 Hopkinson Ave.
Brooklyn, New York
by Zondervan Publishing House

BLACK AND FREE

First printing............July, 1968
Second printing....September, 1968
Third printing........October, 1968
Fourth printing.....November, 1968

Library of Congress Catalog Card Number 68-27459

Printed in the United States of America

Foreword

Here is a book that will challenge and encourage Negroes. It will both shame and inspire white evangelical Christians.

With all the timeliness of today's newspaper, Tom Skinner blasts the myths on both sides of the color spectrum with candor and intellectual honesty.

He has the uncanny ability to put his finger on the root cause of the race problem and at the same time is able to outline an ultimate solution that is amazing. His style is that of a realist, not afraid to tell the truth, even when the truth is painful.

Everyone needs to read this book!

And then, black and white alike, we need to act on what we have found, destroying hate and prejudice on both sides.

Tom's discovery is not new. Jesus Christ gave us the formula for harmonious living some two thousand years ago when He told us to "love one another, even as I have loved you." But Tom's application of that discovery is pure genius.

— THE PUBLISHERS

Introduction

Poverty. Ghettos and slums.

Civil disobedience . . . marches . . . demonstrations.

These are words that have been worked "overtime" in American vocabularies in recent years.

Newspapers are filled — almost daily — with reports on integration, equal opportunity, demonstrations, sit-in's, school bussing plans, riots, looting and violence.

Industry and governments are spending millions of dollars on social action, legislation, and every conceivable means to try and solve the problem of the American Negro.

And almost everyone who has discussed this problem, has a point of view as to how to cope with it. There are as many "solutions" as people.

Government has one idea as to how it should be solved; industry has another. The Democratic party has one plan; the Republican party has another. The White Citizen's Council has an idea; the Black Nationalists have another. From every quarter the arguments are heated, the debates are long and drawn out. How do you solve the problem of race? How do you meet the tremendous responsibilities of poverty? How do you reach the ghetto kid and communicate with him? How do you help those who are born without hope, frustrated and mixed up?

Without being so presumptuous as to claim I have all the solutions to the many problems, I do think that I, as a Negro from the ghetto, have found the most practical, reasonable and sensible solution. That's what this book is all about. It was not written by a man looking at it from the government's point of view, or the church's point of view, or the viewpoint of any religious organization. It does not have a racist, segregationist, or integrationist point of view. It is simply the point of view of a man born and raised in the largest Negro ghetto in America, who has lived with and seen slums. Drug addiction, prostitution, alcoholism, and broken homes are a part of this life. It is the viewpoint of a man who has been exposed to the frustration of a group of people who feel that there is no hope for them, who feel that they are socially rejected, who have been brainwashed into thinking they could never reach a level of acceptability in the United States. It's written by a man who was born black, born with many of the frustrations that a Negro born in the slum area grows up with.

The solutions set forth are the solutions this man has found to bring hope and stability to his own life. This book is for the more than 22 million Negroes in this country, many of them frustrated because they were born black. It is dedicated to those who have experienced poverty, hunger, and the hate of racists.

It is also written for those Negroes who have grown so bitter that they seek to take their frustration out on society. And, it is also written for those professionals, working diligently to solve these many problems. It is also written for the evangelical Christian church in America, which I believe has failed desperately to come to grips with these problems.

It is my hope that as you read this book you will not draw hasty conclusions from its early pages. Please keep from drawing any conclusions until you have finished reading, approaching it with an open mind, to see yourself in the pages of this book.

It is to those who want truth, to those who want hope, to those realists who like to face reality that this book has been written.

—TOM SKINNER

Contents

BLACK AND FREE

Part of Tom Skinner's ministry is communicating to fellows who are very much as he used to be — winning their confidence, and then communicating his faith in Jesus Christ as an alternative to their frustrations.

1

Rumbles in Harlem

It was a little past nine on a hot summer night in July. Word came to us that the Imperial Gang from the Washington Heights District of Manhattan was planning an invasion of our neighborhood — the turf that belonged to the Harlem Lords.

Harlem is overlooked by a hill known as Washington Heights. If you stand on Edgecomb Avenue, you look down some 150 feet into what is called "The Valley." The Imperial Gang operated in the Washington Heights District, between 145th and 155th Streets. The Harlem Lords controlled the neighboring turf between 145th and 155th Streets in "The Valley" between Bradhurst Avenue and the Harlem River.

There's a certain kind of feeling that comes over you just before a rumble. It has the anticipation of an exciting football or basketball game, but with the nagging fear that a soldier experiences on his way to the front lines. Everyone was afraid — deep inside — but even more frightened to show it.

The Imperial Gang is a large one. It's gained quite a reputation for being able to take on other gangs and defeat them.

This wasn't my first gang rumble, but it was the first time I had led the Harlem Lords. I had strategically taken the fellows — a little over 115 of them — into 150th Street between Bradhurst Avenue and Eighth Avenue. At Bradhurst Avenue and 150th Street there was a park. About thirty or forty yards into that park began some steps that led all the way up the hill onto Edgecomb Avenue into what was known as the Hill District of Washington Heights.

I sent a number of the fellows of our gang up 145th Street, one approach to the hill. I sent another group of fellows up 155th Street, (known as the viaduct), just opposite the Polo Grounds where the New York Giants used to play baseball. That was the other exit leading into the Hill District. And then I planted a group of fellows in the basements along 150th Street between Bradhurst and Eighth Avenues. Several fellows were located on top of the roofs six stories up with pellet guns. Finally, a group of the fellows stood in the open in the street while I hid in one of the cars, directing the fellows from the car.

I had gained the reputation for being quite a gang strategist because I was in a special advanced class that met after school where we studied ancient and modern military tactics. I took the various strategies the field generals used in open field battles all the way back from primitive Greece to modern day times. I'd modify them, make them applicable to street fights so we wouldn't lose. If I succeeded in leading the fellows to victory in this particular fight, I'd emerge as the leader of the most powerful teenage gang in the city.

Suddenly the word came from one of the fellows on top of the roof that the Imperial Gang had been spotted at the top of Edgecomb Avenue and they were beginning to come down the steps.

They saw ten or twenty of our fellows in the open, thinking that was all there was to the gang. This rumble would be a fast and easy one, they must have reasoned. As soon as they got down into the streets, the twenty fellows on the street began to back up, luring them even further into the main street. Then, our guys ran and the fellows we had planted on the rooftops began to fire pellet guns down into the streets.

The Imperial gang sought cover in the basements where we had fellows planted. Our guys crashed bottles across their heads as they came through the doorways, opening gaping wounds and knocking some unconscious.

The surprised Imperials found swinging, angry members of the Harlem Lords surrounding them. The sultry summer air rang with shouts and screams of pain. Here and there you could see black faces livid with bright red blood where a bottle or bicycle chain had done its nasty work.

Now it was time for the kill.

The Imperials had been chased into our area and we were going to mop them up. I got out of the car and surged after the nearest Imperial. In one hand I had a homemade blackjack — a lead ball in an old sock. I swung it and heard a sickening crunch as it smashed down on the head of the unsuspecting Imperial. In my other hand was a set of brass knuckles, carefully fitted to my fist. They flashed out in the dark night. I felt the wetness of blood and sweat as my fist connected with the face of another Imperial.

Someone yelled, "Tom! Look out!"

Instinctively I ducked, just as a bottle flew past my head.

I grabbed my would-be attacker and knocked him to the pavement with a single swing of my brass-knuckled fist. Before he could get up I stomped heavily into his stomach. His eyes rolled and he passed out. Other Imperials were screaming in pain, some screaming defiance as they retreated. They had been beaten!

As I revelled in my newly won status, the piercing sirens of converging squad cars warned us the police had been alerted.

In forty different directions my gang members fled, disappearing down alleys, into homes, and away from the rumble.

As I ran, I looked back at the litter of bricks, clubs, bleeding and unconscious Imperials, and broken bottles. The Imperials were beaten — I was The Big Man!

2

Why Do They Fight?

Many of my white friends can't understand what causes a youth to rumble, to savagely take out his frustrations in gang fights that brutally maim and scar and sometimes kill.

What's it all about?

What leads to gang warfare? What makes people in Harlem, in Watts, the south side of Chicago, the east side of Detroit, the south side of Philadelphia, or the Hill district of Pittsburgh get involved in this kind of thing?

And in particular, people across America are asking, "Why do Negroes riot?"

Yet, most of them really know the answer. It's the ghetto. And to better understand the frustration and bitterness that fosters gang wars and riots, we have to look beyond the slums themselves. In fact, we need to go back some three hundred years — to when the first slaves were brought to this country. They were imported from Africa via the West Indies.

These unsuspecting and unprotected Africans were captured and snatched away from their country and culture, from their own language and people, and shipped like so many animals to America as a form of cheap labor.

Expeditions would arrive at African seaports with a load of slaves. The men were separated from the women and the more sickly were usually killed on the spot with a quick thrust of a sword. They were packed — often as many as a hundred — in a small hold of the slave ship. Here they remained, locked and chained in the cramped, smelly brig for the entire voyage There were no facilities for sanitation and human excrement. Things were so bad that the crew members couldn't go near the hold. They poured a slop of food scraps down the hatch over the hold. Meanwhile, the slaves were all but out of their minds. Not used to confinement, frightened and seasick, weak from lack of food and water, and cramped in the tiny hold, they fought and madly tried to climb out of the hold whenever it was opened for "feeding time."

Some of the stalwart survived the trip. Many, many were lost.

Those that did survive were sold on the auction block. The plantation owners and farmers bought Negroes as easily and disinterestedly as they would buy a draft horse or milk cow. To the planter, the Negro was just another animal to be used on his farm or plantation.

The slave was nothing more than just a physical animal. He was bred at the whims of his master. Whenever his master felt there was a need for additional slaves, he merely selected a healthy male and a healthy female and he had them cohabit until a child was conceived. When the woman was pregnant the man was moved to other quarters to impregnate another woman. On and on went the pattern, so that within ten years, a slave male could have sired more than a hundred sons and daughters, but never really have the privilege of fathering any of them.

It was in this climate that the slave was looked upon as sub-human. His women were raped freely at the whims of the slave master, and whenever a master had guests in his home who came from distant places it was considered part of hospitality to offer any one of the slave women to sleep with that man for the night.

There was no family life; there was no culture, no discipline set up as far as a home was concerned during all the

17

three hundred years that the Negro was in slavery in this country.

Within a matter of a hundred years or so, slavery in the United States became an economic way of life, sanctioned by some of the most noble, the most elite, the most legal, philosophical, legislative minds of our land. It soon began to be argued by even the church that slavery was a divine institution ordained by God. Others quoted Scripture, from the book of Genesis, of how Ham was cursed and how through Noah his children were all given a low position. "Why," they said, "the word 'Ham' even means black." They argued that all black people had been relegated by God to a condition of slavery, to serve the white man for the rest of his life. Therefore, they reasoned, "God has ordained it to be so," and as one individual wrote from Texas not too long ago, "Woe be unto any white man that seeks to raise a black man out of the condition that God has cursed him."

This became the philosophy; this became the way of life.

Only a few showed any concern at all for the slaves.

Some people within the evangelical churches urged that the slaves should be taught the Bible and be offered Christ's redemption. They wanted the slave to know that Christ died for the black man, too. But the overwhelming majority of people in the Christian world preached that the Negro was sub-human; he didn't have a soul anyway, so Christ couldn't have died for him. Therefore, it wasn't necessary for him to hear the Gospel.

What little the slave heard about Christianity, about the message of Jesus Christ, came as a result of the few privileged slaves who were able to accompany their masters to church on Sunday morning. They were able to sit outside the windows or climb up into one of the lofts on top of the church building and peek through one of the holes and hear the preacher preach. And what the slave could glean from that meeting he would take back to the slave quarters.

It was out of this that some of the spirituals developed.

Thus some inkling of the message of Jesus Christ was able to infiltrate the slave camps of the South.

These fragments of the Christian faith were the only particles of hope to which the Negro could cling. His entire existence was shrouded in hopelessness. Slavery continued for three hundred years in America. Generation after generation was born in the gloom and utter despondency of slavery.

But late in the eighteenth century and early in the nineteenth century, cries of liberation, cries of freedom began to come from the more liberal elements of the land. More and more from the north came tremendous clamors for liberty, for freedom. Free the slave; give him his right to take his place in society. Give him his right to live; give him his right to become an adequate human being.

And they began to preach. The constitution stated that all men were born with certain inalienable rights. More insistently came the cries until finally the Civil War came, splitting the Union.

President Lincoln issued the famous Emancipation Proclamation, and the slaves were set free!

After three hundred years of captivity, the Negro was suddenly a free individual. He was told, "Now that you have your freedom, now that you have been emancipated, you must assume responsibility as a human being. You must now become a responsible citizen."

They turned to this man who was bred like cattle, who perhaps did not even *know* his children, and asked him to raise his family.

Three hundred years separated the Negro from life in a family culture. He had never been shown or taught what it was to have family responsibility, to be the head of his own home.

Overnight, the Negro was told now that he was a free man, he must live according to the culture he served and by their standards.

Suddenly he was taught that he must live with one wife and raise and teach his children.

Children who never knew what it was to have a father were suddenly told they must honor, obey, and respect their parents.

So began this tremendous period of "reconstruction" in American history.

During this so-called Reconstruction Era, the American Negro tried hard to assimilate into American cultural society. He began a program of self-help and self-determination. Such philosophies were advanced by men like Booker T. Washington — pull yourself up by your boot straps, they argued. Help yourself, learn to use your hands, go out and work and dig and build for yourself. And throughout the South began a tremendous movement by which Negroes began to seek to pull themselves up by their boot straps, purchase their own land, build their own homes, father their own children, and to become responsible, respectable men.

In 1871 the first Negro senator, elected from the state of Mississippi no less, was elected to the United States Senate. In 1875, another one came from Virginia, another followed from Alabama, and the Negro began to make tremendous strides. He began to build his own churches; he soon developed lawyers, politicians, educators, teachers, leaders.

But as the Negro pushed, his progress became a threat to a very large segment of society in America, particularly to the poor white in the South. You see, it was the poor white who saw that if the Negro continued to advance at the rate he was going, he would become a threat to his own superior position. He would no longer have anybody to look down upon, so cries of "Let's keep the Negroes in their place," "Let's not let them go too far too fast," were sounded. Pulled from the past was old religious philosophy that God had cursed the Negro and relegated him to a condition of servitude. Up went the cries and soon it began to be heard again from the pulpits of America. Pastors began to preach and religious leaders began to plead, "Don't mongrelize the races! If we allow the Negroes to have any more progress, it will end up mongrelizing the races."

Thus began an intense program of persecution in the

South against the American Negro, the former slave, this man who was now supposed to be free, to put him "in his place."

The Negro could come home in the evening from a hard day's work and find crosses burning on his lawn. Or he could return in the evening and find that his wife had been raped. He would be forced to stand in his home with guns pointed at him while men took turns savagely raping his wife. Although "free," the Negro was subject to every kind of indignity one can imagine.

He was not given the right to vote. All kinds of laws were passed to make it difficult, if not impossible, for the Negro to go to the polls. Any Negro who exercised leadership within the Negro community, who sought to gain for the Negro the opportunity to assimilate into American cultural society, with all the rights and privileges that belong to this growth, soon found himself stopped. He wasn't able to buy food in any store; no credit was extended to him; his home was soon burned. He found that because he wasn't able to keep certain legal papers, that banks and lawyers were working out schemes to take his property away. Any inheritance that came to him from some gracious white person was taken away. Finally, the Negro found himself returning to a condition that was worse than slavery.

And yet with all this persecution, people kept wondering why didn't the Negro change? Why didn't he become any better? Why didn't he move to a nicer place? Why didn't he keep up his home? Why didn't he get a better job? Why wasn't he better educated, more cultured, more refined?

Between 1900 and 1910 an epidemic of lynchings began in the South. Negroes were taken out and killed for no reason at all. Some were shot on such ridiculous charges as standing too close on the street to a white person or being too friendly with a white person. Others were killed for staring at a white woman too long. He was being shot, whipped, and lynched at the whim of the whites. His home might be burned for the slightest "offense" to white society.

21

Then came World War I. Some Negroes went off to fight. Tales began to come back from some of the Negroes who were able to see other cities like New York, Chicago, Detroit, Cleveland. The word was that here was a better place to live. There were opportunities in many of these northern cities that the Negro could never dream of having in the South. These cities became the "promised land" for the Negro. The cries went up throughout the South, "There are jobs and better living in the North! Go to New York, go to Cleveland, go to Detroit, go to Los Angeles; make your way to Chicago — you'll find a better way of life!"

And so in the early 20's there began small migrations of Negro families to the North. It built up during the depression period until the mid-thirties, and World War II brought even more.

One of those cities termed "the promised land," one of the cities that was depicted throughout the South to the American Negro as being a land of hope, a land of prosperity, a land of freedom, was the city of New York. Parents looking for a better way of life for themselves and their children packed what little belongings they had, left their farms, and began a long trip north to "the promised land," New York City. Most of them migrated to that little community known as Harlem.

In 1940, just after their marriage, my parents were among those who took the trip north to find a better life in "the promised land." I was born June 6, 1942, two years before D-Day. It was pitch black in New York City. New York City was undergoing a blackout and I was told that I was born under candlelight. There begins my story.

3

Introducing Tom Skinner

It was into this community of Harlem that I was born. I grew up two blocks from the Polo Grounds where the New York Giants used to play baseball.

I was born into a fairly religious home — religious to the extent that my father was and is a minister, but that was about it. You see, to me, church was something you were supposed to do because it was a fine, respectable thing to do. But religion, or Christianity, never made too much sense to me. In fact, most of the people I met who claimed to be Christians showed glaring contradictions in their lives.

I looked at the kind of community Harlem was and I couldn't reconcile it with the kind of Christianity I knew in my own home and church.

As you may know, New York City is divided into five boroughs — the Bronx, Brooklyn, Queens, Staten Island, and Manhattan. Manhattan is the center of activity in New York. It's where the Empire State Building is, the New York Stock Exchange, Broadway — the Great White Way, Rockefeller Center, theatres, bright lights, Times Square, the so-called crossroads of life in America.

As you proceed north from Manhattan, you pass through Central Park. Where Central Park ends — about 110th Street, near Lenox Avenue — Harlem begins.

Harlem is a heavily-populated Negro ghetto. It has become a synonym for any of the Negro communities around the world.

Harlem is a small community geographically. It's a rectangle that is about two and one-half miles long and a mile wide. Yet, crammed into that tiny box of real estate are more than a million people. You don't realize the significance of this overcrowding until you read where social statisticians tell us that if you took the entire population of the United States — all 200 million of us — and concentrated it into the five boroughs of New York City, it would still not be as congested as Harlem.

This was my birthplace. Here I was raised to learn and grow to take my place in the American culture. My playground was a vacant lot with broken bottles and rusty tin cans and an abandoned auto.

Harlem then was more than 70 per cent slums. People lived in rat infested, run down homes that the landlords never cared for. People paid outrageously high rents for places that were nothing more than rat-traps. It was not uncommon to wake up in the middle of the night and hear the piercing scream of a mother as she discovered her two-month-old baby had been gnawed to death by a large rat.

You could set your watch as to when the police would drive into the neighborhood to collect their bribes to keep racketeering alive. Mike, the local racketeer, on a pre-set time every afternoon would step out of his candy store which was a front for local gambling. A patrol car would turn in the block and two policemen would park, get out, go around the corner, while Mike dropped a large brown paper bag in the back of the squad car and stepped back, having paid his bribe for that day to maintain his racketeering.

Half the children in Harlem born since World War II were born out of wedlock. More than half of them grow up without their fathers, producing what the sociologists call a matriarchal problem, which simply means that the child's father is never home. And this problem, as I saw with my own eyes, produces several effects.

First, if an adolescent grows up in Harlem without the devotion, the care, the affection, the discipline of a father, it means that he is raised by his mother. If his mother is the strong, domineering type of woman, she controls the boy to such an extreme that when he becomes an early teenager, he leans toward homosexuality. He identifies aggressiveness and domination not with his father, because he has no father with whom to relate. Instead, he relates aggressiveness with his mother. And he feels that in order to be aggressive and strong and domineering, he has to act like his mother. All of his mother's preconceived ideas about sex standards, morality, and ethics are computed in the way he acts and conducts himself. If, on the other hand, she is not a strong domineering, forceful type, she loses that boy by the time he is 13 or 14. He takes to the streets for identity. Her only resort in controlling him is to seek to degrade him, to make him feel bad, hoping that that will put him in line. And she makes such statements as, "You're getting worse every day. You're ending up to be no good, just like your no-good old man." And every time he does something wrong, he is reminded of his "no-good old man" who ran off and left his mother when he was three years old.

So he grows up hating his father. In fact, he grows up hating any type of male leadership and any time he sees male leadership, there is only one reaction against it — to rebel, whether that authority is his school teacher or whether it is the police. He rebels against *any* type of male authority.

The kid doesn't know what it's like to have a father take him to the ball game, or on a picnic, or to take a family vacation. The average youngster in Harlem doesn't even know what a vacation is all about. A vacation to him is the two months you don't go to school, but even then, he never goes outside his community. He's never seen the countryside. He doesn't even know what a real cow looks like.

To compound this matriarchal problem is the fact that the majority of the school teachers, principals, and assistant principals in the Harlem community are women. Boys grow up with nothing but woman domination around them. Whenever a teacher wants to reprimand him for becoming a disciplinary problem, the reaction usually is, "George, what's wrong with you? Why can't you act any better? Hasn't your father taught you any better?" How that hurts. He doesn't *have* a father, and his resentment builds and builds.

If this teenager is a girl, she grows up wanting to be like her mother, keeping "the old man" in his place. Sometimes the very domineering type of woman does have the husband around, but he's henpecked. He doesn't have a decent job. The mother has to go out to help make a living, and as the person who brings home the check, she ends up running things. The girl grows up watching her mother dominate her father, putting him in his place. He's just another roomer in the house. He actually isn't a part of the decision-making of the household, and so the girl grows up saying, "You know, I want to be just like my mother." She wants to grow up being a domineering type of person — what we call on the streets of Harlem a "billy-girl." She never grows out of her tomboy stage and by the time she's eighteen and other girls are wearing dresses and seeking to look nice and to keep themselves up, she's still dressed in dungarees, got her hair cut short — a tough-looking, hard-as-nails woman.

But some girls say, "I'm not going to be like my mother. I'm not going to marry the kind of man that I can push around. I'm going to marry a *real* man." Of course, her concept of a real man is the kind of man who, when she gets out of line, socks her in the jaw, and knocks some of her teeth out. She always looks bad from cuts and bruises from this "real" man's fists. To her, that's the only concept of masculinity.

Understandably, the average Negro girl born and raised in Harlem under these circumstances is born and raised with a very distorted idea of manhood.

Many of the girls, just for sense of status, will go out and have sexual relations with a boy in order to become pregnant by him. Unlike her white counterpart, the Negro girl *wants* to be a mother.

All she wants from the boy, however, is the "status" of being a mother. Once she has the child, she no longer needs the boy — in fact, has no use for him whatsoever. In this confused and distorted community of mixed values and obscured standards, her goal in life is to be a mother because it's an accomplishment she can attain. It's something she sees within her reach and she doesn't care how she gets it. To her, being a mother gives her a sense of fulfillment and prestige.

The results of the matriarchal society have been probably the most damning thing to come out of the ghetto.

It is a vicious cycle that brings children into the world knowing only the domineering influence of the woman — and girls whose only aspiration is to bring other children into the world.

There is no real discipline and no values for the vast majority of Harlem's young people. We grew up in the midst of growing bitterness, resentment, distrust and poverty. Normal relationships, family relationships, were totally unknown to most of us.

Today, there are more than *sixty thousand* dope addicts in Harlem. They are supporting habits that cost them from fifty to one hundred dollars a day. Obviously, they can't obtain money legally to support a habit costing that much. Some of the men rob; others are burglars, car thieves, or pushers who recruit new addicts. The girls — often finding themselves "hooked" on heroin by age fourteen begin to pay for their narcotics by acting as lookout for one of the men burglarizing a house or store. Or a girl might try shoplifting. But the narcotics give less and less of a "kick" each time. She needs more. And it costs more. The only way to get a lot of money in a hurry is through prostitution. If she's young, she may earn as much as $150.00 a day. If she's old — and a prostitute is *old at 25* — she won't do as well.

Dope, prostitution, gambling, extortion, rape, murder, sex

crimes, robbery, poverty, rats, stench, overcrowding. These were the everyday sights, sounds and smells I had growing up in Harlem.

Harlem is best described as hell on earth.

And there was no escaping it.

There, if you like, is a *cause* . . . a. reason . . . a *"why?"* for Negro problems.

4

Where Do They Fail?

As a teenager, I looked around and asked my father where God was in all this? I couldn't for the life of me see how God, if He cared for humanity at all, could allow the conditions that existed in Harlem.

There were whites who made a lot of noise about how God was the answer to all our problems and how the Bible was our hope.

Perhaps this *hyper-Christian* did more to turn me from Christ than bring me to Him. This fellow had the sum total of the Negro problem neatly packaged in a quaint little platitude. And he offered it freely. It was a vocal pat on the head and token "be of good cheer." This fellow called himself, and I quote, "a Bible-believing orthodox fundamental conservative evangelical Christian" (whatever that means).

Basically, this individual had a half dozen Bible verses for every social problem that existed. If you went to him and told him that a place like Harlem existed, he would say, "Well, what those people up there need is a good dose of salvation." That all sounded well and good, except for the fact that I never saw the fellow actually in Harlem administering that "dose of salvation."

If you told him that there are more than 60,000 drug addicts in Harlem, his reaction would be, "Well, those people up there need to hear the Gospel, need to be born again."

This is true. But I never saw him in Harlem communicating the message of the new birth and pointing people to Jesus Christ.

If you told him about the conditions of Harlem, he would cry out with typical piety, "Christ is the answer!"

But this fellow who called himself a "Bible-believing orthodox fundamental conservative evangelical" Christian withdrew himself into the cloistered walls of his particular church or denomination, and somehow we never heard *how* "Christ is the answer!"

This hyper-Christian took great pride in "holding on to New Testament truth," while all the liberals and the modernists "are contaminating the Word of God" and denying the virgin birth and the resurrection of Christ. He considered himself one of the last group really holding on to the fundamental truth.

But he was choking on that fundamental truth. He should have taken that truth out into the mainstream of everyday life and made Jesus Christ relevant to the drug addict, the alcoholic, that individual who is down and out.

He never once ventured into a community like Harlem to preach Jesus Christ. To the shame of so-called white evangelical Christianity in this country, they have neglected one of the most significant, one of the most fruitful mission fields in the world — the American Negro.

This attitude holds for Chicago, it holds for the Watts District of Los Angeles, for Harlem, for Brooklyn, for the Hill District of Pittsburgh, for the south and north sides of Philadelphia, that wherever there are strong heavy populations of Negro people, the white conservative, evangelical Christian in this country has fled.

There are certain evangelical Christians who take great pride in the fact that they don't have anything to do with the people who are of liberal theological persuasion. They take great pride in the fact that they are "separated" from them. They're always seeking to defend themselves against being "contaminated" by liberal theology. And yet, when the neighborhood where their church is located begins to change and Negroes begin to move in, they take off. And although they would have no prior dealing with "modernists," they will turn around and sell that church in order to get out of the community. They sell quickly to some liberal group or some Negro cult group in order to salve their consciences and get out of the community. *And the story is the same in every Negro ghetto in this country!*

Wherever Negroes have moved in, whites have packed up and moved out. They take with them their evangelical churches and witness. So today we're finding ourselves with large cities heavily populated by minority groups, but no sound, evangelical Gospel to preach them at all.

And what about this man who claims that Jesus Christ is the answer? With heart tinged with emotion, he packs his bags and takes the next boat to Africa, to reach the black man with the Gospel. He spends millions of dollars to reach that black man. He crosses the Atlantic and Pacific Oceans, he flies, he goes through all kinds of sacrifices; he'll contract malaria; he'll get shot; he'll lose his own children in order to go to the mission field to reach the black man in Africa with the Gospel.

But he won't cross the street. He won't spend a quarter to go to the other side of town to reach a group of people with the same black skin, who are nowhere near as primitive, and where there is *no* language barrier.

To the shame of the so-called white, evangelical, conservative Christian in the United States, he does not support financially, morally, spiritually or in any other way, works that are attempting to communicate the message of Jesus Christ to the Negro in America.

There is virtually no attempt to reach this vast number of black people in America who are hopeless and frustrated and want a way out.

I grew up, although a preacher's son, ignorant of the real Gospel. Our Christianity taught that Christ was a good man to pattern your life after. But the pattern was so remote and fragile that I put my concept of Christ on a pedestal. I never envisioned Christ as a Person who could change and direct the course of my life.

I had nothing but a distorted picture of Christianity, and as a teenager I said, "Listen, if Christianity is real, it's not for me."

There is hardly any Christian witness in the ghetto.

It's not surprising that something comes in to fill this void. During my teen years, and even today, that void is being filled by militant black nationalists who give the ghetto man a cause to rally around, a pride to fight for. They are the ones preaching black supremacy — the very opposite of the White Citizen's Council or the Ku Klux Klan.

Day after day, very candidly these fellows said to me, "Tom, your problem is that you have been brainwashed. You have been educated and trained and brought up under Christianity which is nothing more than a white man's religion given to the Negro in order to keep him in his place." And they pointed out that any progressive colored kid who wanted to get ahead would reject any concept of Christianity as being neo-colonialistic, old fashioned, and out of date. They argued that while the white man would teach the Negro to love him, to love his neighbor, to love God, to have patience, to be humble, he would teach him only while he had his foot on the black man's neck. He would preach to him about love while denying him the right to a decent job. He urged the Negro to obey God's Word while raping his women. He was telling him to love God and country although his home was burning, his family shot and his property destroyed.

All they said was true. History records it all.

They kept feeding me this kind of information day after day. They pointed out to me that some of the leading exponents of hate, segregation, and bigotry in American society were in Bible-believing churches. They reminded me that the most segregated hour in American society was eleven o'clock on Sunday morning.

As they gave me this kind of information, day after day, I grew more and more bitter.

It was this idea as a teenager that the nationalists kept feeding me and feeding me and feeding me until I grew bitter with the whole concept of Christianity. They showed me how hypocritical the entire system was. They gave me information in writing where some of the major denominations in this country actually had in their constitutions that the Negro did not need to hear the Gospel of Jesus Christ because he was sub-human. Other churches still have in their constitutions today that a Negro is not to be admitted as a member of that particular church.

There are a number of churches with which I am supposed to be associated that would never have me in their church. The congregation wouldn't allow me to break bread with them; wouldn't allow me to preach or speak on their platforms *for no other reason than the fact that I am a Negro.*

At the peak of my resentment and bitterness, I was coming home from school one afternoon and I was approached by a young fellow I recognized as a member of one of the gangs in the Harlem community. Very sarcastically he approached me and said, "Hey, Tom. How would you like to belong to the Harlem Lords?" That was the name of his gang. Of course, he was being very facetious because he knew I was a preacher's kid. And if you know anything about preacher's kids, we're supposed to be nice, innocent fellows who don't bother anyone.

But I took him up on it.

"Yeah, man. I'd like to belong."

"You're puttin' me on, dad . . ."

"No," I replied. Deep down inside myself I had to prove to the fellows that just because I was a preacher's kid didn't mean I couldn't be as tough as the rest of them.

"In order to be a member of the Harlem Lords you gotta pass the initiation test," he cautioned. "We'll see if you're tough enough to be in the gang!"

5

The Harlem Lords

I

That night I met the Harlem Lords. Or, should I say they met *me?*

I don't know if they saw through me, but I was scared. The only thing that helped me go through with it was my resolve to show everyone that I was as tough as they. Three of the older gang members came up to me. The leader — whom I'll call Joseph — looked at me with eyes that bored right through me.

"So you wanna be a member of the Lords?"

I nodded.

"You think you got what it takes?"

Again I nodded.

There was ragged laughter as some of those sitting nearby heard the remarks of Joseph. He raised his hand for quiet.

"You know, you gotta pass the initiation test, don't you?"

"Name it," I said with a cocky snarl.

"We gonna be nice to you, Skinner. We gonna give you three choices."

"Go ahead . . ."

"You choose whatever one you want. Choice number one . . . we'll strip you to the waist, tie your hands and hang you from the spike." He pointed to a brick wall where a long spike had been cemented in. The alley would then become an arena with everyone watching one of the bigger gang members beat me with a leather and rope lash some twenty times.

"And if you cry out, you won't be tough enough for the Lords."

"Tell 'im what the other choices are," someone yelled from the darkness.

Joseph continued, "Second choice is this. We'll pick two guys to jump on you and beat you 'til they get tired or until you get knocked out. You'll take what they dish out without fighting back and without asking them to stop."

I licked my lips and became conscious of the dryness of my mouth. When I spoke, my voice was just above a whisper. "And what's my third choice?"

"For the third choice, you turn and face this brick wall. Then we'll take Sammy here and put him right beside you. We'll give Sammy his knife and blindfold him. Then he'll take ten steps, turn and throw the knife where he thinks you are. If he misses, you'll be a member of the Lords. If he doesn't miss, you won't have to worry about it, will you?" asked Joseph with eyes flashing, eager for the test to begin. I looked into his face, one scarred and mutilated by many rumbles and wondered how my own face would look in a few years of street fighting — if I passed my initiation and lived that long.

I chose the first test — the lashes.

Roughly they tied my hands in front of me and lifted me to hang from the giant spike. Other hands clawed at my shirt and tore it from my back. I flexed the muscles in my shoulders and back and clamped my teeth down hard to await the blows.

I heard the wind sound made by the lash as it whipped through the still night air. No one was talking now. No laughing. It hit! With the pain of tearing flesh and bruised muscles, the lash struck once.

Still there was silence except for the grunt of the tall

gang member swinging the lash and the sound of the whip itself. *Two!*

It was pain upon pain as the whip struck the welts raised by the first blow. It took every ounce of self-control to keep from crying out. *Three!*

The pain caused my arms and shoulders to quiver uncontrollably as a reflex action to shake off the lashes. *Four!* — or was it five? I lost track quickly and tried to take my mind off the beating.

Finally it was over. My head was aching and my senses reeling. Two of the fellows cut me down and I struggled to stand. I tried to manage a cocky grin. "Is that twenty already?"

"Yeah," Joseph grinned back. "Why? You wanna go again?"

"Not just today."

That broke the ice and the laughter and talking started up again. Now the sarcasm was gone. In its place, genuine friendship. Out of the hate of that initiation was born a strange kind of affection that binds a boy to the gang.

I had done it. I had taken their punishment and passed the test. I was now a member of the Harlem Lords!

II

After six weeks of fighting with the Harlem Lords, getting involved in several rumbles, breaking into a few stores and doing some other stealing, I sized up the leader of our gang. I decided, "Why should I be just a member of the gang when I can be the *leader?*"

To be top man, you merely challenge the current leader. The two of you decide what weapons will be used. The choice is varied. We could fight barehanded, relying on brute force. We could duel with clubs, using garbage can lids as shields. Or we could use knives.

We decided on a knife duel.

Again the animal interest in the combat between men. The two of us squared off in a garbage-littered alley with the rest of the gang looking on. A tiny ray of light danced off the edge of his blade as he swung it past my face. As I pulled back, my own arm reached out and arched toward his belly. My blade only creased his shirt, tearing it slightly.

After several thrusts by each of us, we became more wary. Jabs were more cautious and more carefully aimed. He faked a thrust toward my neck, quickly flipping his knife to the other hand to stab me in the stomach. But he wasn't quite fast enough. I dodged his swing and drove my own knife into his side as I whirled.

He dropped to his knees, holding his side in apparent disbelief. Blood was streaming through his fingers as he nodded to me that he was finished.

The Harlem Lords had a new leader!

For two years I would reign as undisputed leader of the gang.

When some people hear this sort of thing described, they think, "Well, how barbaric can these teenagers be?" But how little it occurs to the average sophisticated American that the same kind of rat race for social status and leadership goes on in our world today.

All of us are conformists to a certain extent. We all have a particular in-group or social society that we look to for acceptance. Whether it's a women's special tea group that you want to belong to as a lady; a country club as a man; whether it's the guys in the office you're trying to get in with or the kids on campus; everybody on every social level seeks to belong to some clique, circle or "in" group.

A kid born in a Negro ghetto is no different. A majority of the kids his age say that the only way you can be accepted by others is to be a member of the gang. So, he fights to belong, if the gang says that's the only way they can look up to him. The only person they recognize with any status, prestige, or power is the individual who leads this gang. You want prestige and power, so you fight to become leader. It's the same rat race on every social level. It's the same desire to belong.

And many people depict gang leaders as a bunch of mentally retarded, uncouth, or punch-drunk fellows who don't know how to talk or don't know how to act. They envision them with bandanas around their heads, with dirty sneakers and dungarees.

But just to set the record straight, while I was leader of the gang, I was also president of the student body at school. I was a member of the Arista Society, made up of the cream of the intellectual crop. I was president of the Shakespearean Club. And I was a member of the baseball team. I was also president of the young people's department in my own church. By the time I was fourteen years of age, I'd acted out full length plays of Shakespeare, Hamlet, and Macbeth, playing the title roles. So I wasn't *too* mentally retarded.

The second reason that I found myself belonging to the gang was that these same black nationalists under whose influence I had come said to me, "Tom, it's a fine thing that you're a student leader, that you're getting good marks at school, and that you show the qualifications of leadership. If you've got any idea about making it in our kind of world, you'd better think again. If you've got any idea about getting ahead in our kind of society, then you'd better let us school you again. You see Tom, this is a white man's world. He controls things from the top to the bottom.

"He might allow you to be a jazz player, a rock-and-roll singer, or the janitor in his building. But he will never allow you to compete with him on an open basis to make a tangible contribution to American society. He feels you are inferior to him. He is convinced that you could never be his equal. He believes somehow that you will never reach the level of social, cultural, intellectual society that he has reached. He will always look down upon you.

"And Tom, you may be able to make thirty thousand dollars a year and want to move into the best of communities, but as soon as you try to move in, he will protest loudly at all kinds of council meetings to try to keep you out. If you do move in he will ignore you. When your children go out on the street to play he will call his kids in because he's afraid that at four years of age they just might want to intermarry. He doesn't want you living next door to him because you might mongrelize the races. You see, Tom, he doesn't *want* you. You've got to accept that, Tom."

And this is what they said to me day after day. "You are not accepted by him as your equal. You might as well give up any idea about intellectual pursuits, about making it in our kind of world, and join the rebellion — join the revolution. Put the white man in his place. Get him back."

They presented to me the convincing evidence that there were outstanding men in Negro society with great ability, great intellectual power, and tremendous talent and gifts who were not allowed to develop to the fullest of their potential because of the racist attitudes in American society. And so I grew more bitter and more frustrated. Like a stagnant pond, I backed up on myself. I began to hate the day I was ever born in Harlem and cursed the day that I was ever born black.

And across America, at this very moment, are literally hundreds of thousands of Negro teenagers who face the same frustration. They are becoming the easy prey for the black nationalist or any other militant extremist group who exploit them and turn their bitterness into rebellion.

The Negro is told by them that he doesn't have a decent chance for an education. They tell you to look at a community like the Watts District of Los Angeles, where there isn't one hospital in the whole district. The Watts District of Los Angeles is about the size of Boston, Massachusetts. There's no swimming pool for the kids to use. Then along comes an extremist exploiter who eloquently uses those situations. He takes these situations and bitterness and exploits them for his own benefit. No wonder there's rebellion. No wonder there are riots.

It is not very difficult to get to a group of people who have been made to feel that they are second-class. You can get through to those who have been told that they **can** never accomplish anything and never really compete with the rest of society on an open basis. It is not difficult to get people like that worked up. It wasn't difficult to get *me* worked up.

I admit that the first time I had to get involved in an act of violence, it wasn't easy. The first time I had to break into a store and steal; the first time I had to break a bottle across someone's head; the first time I had to lead the fellows into a gang rumble — these weren't easy because of my moral and ethical upbringing as a preacher's kid.

But there is something very peculiar about that three letter word the Bible calls "sin." If you keep having your own way, defying your own conscience, trying to ignore the fact that there is a God placing claims upon your life; you are soon at the place where your conscience grows hard. You become indifferent and get to the place where you convince yourself that what you think, do, and act is right.

Take, for instance, that drunkard who lies on the street. The first time he was sprawled out on the street stone drunk, that wasn't the first time he drank. It began through a whole series of drinks — one small one, then a bigger one, then a bigger one, until his conscience became insensitive.

Then, there is that girl who has a reputation in the office or school for going to bed with men. It took time for her reputation to grow. It took time for her to commit her first act of immorality, then the second time, then the third time. Now, immorality is a way of life with her.

There was a time when a person who was selfish was an outcast in the community. He wasn't considered normal. But today, selfishness is a philosophy called psychic-selfism.

In other words, what we've done is attune man's conscience to what he's doing.

Just as the racist convinces himself that his racial prejudice is really good for both races, I had gotten to the place where I could take a bottle, bash it across a fellow's head and be undisturbed about it. I could take that same bottle, break it in half, and shove the glass in the man's face and twist it without even batting my eye.

By the time I left the gang I had twenty-two notches on the handle of my knife which meant that my blade had gone into twenty-two different fellows.

All I knew was that I was gripped with a tremendous sense of power. To maintain my status as a gang leader, I had to act tough and to be tough. The only way I could keep the gang in line was for them to respect my leadership. And the only way I could gain respect was to let them know I wasn't afraid to plunge my knife between some guy's ribs.

During this period of time my parents never once knew that I was a gang leader. In fact, every now and then to make things look good, I would have the fellows chase me home. They would give me a head start down the street and take off after me, giving me just enough room to burst into the house out of breath. They would stand outside the door hollering and cursing my name and threatening my life. We gave my parents the impression that I was the poor innocent preacher's kid, victim of my environment. And my poor ignorant parents, like the average teenager's parents in American society, would say, "I don't know what's happening to the neighborhood. Our dear son Tom can't even walk the streets any more."

I know that perhaps there might be some parents reading these pages who will say, "I resent being called ignorant." But you see, the average teenager today has a tremendous advantage over his parents. The average parent makes the mistake of thinking that the sun sets and rises on his children. All too often we have the tendency of communicating to our children our desire for social status. We say to our kids, "Look, do right — not because it's the right thing to do, but because the wrong thing will embarrass me socially."

Often my work has taken me into areas that are not slum areas. I've had to go into the homes of young people who live in the suburban communities of New York City where the combined incomes of their parents are $30,000 a year and up. And these kids have some real problems, too.

They have to wake up on a school day morning and try to figure out which sports car to drive to school and how to spend their $40.00 a week allowance. I would have liked to have had those problems as a teenager!

If I went into that kid's home and presented his parents with evidence that their son was involved in a drug ring or some sex ring in town, I would almost get kicked out of the home as that parent would tell me, "Not my George." "Not my Sue." "Don't you understand, Mr. Skinner? We're in the social register. We've raised our kids to be more socially respectable than that."

Some time ago I was invited up to Mount Vernon, New York, in Westchester County. Some of the responsible people in that city were concerned about the fact that every Thursday night young people from all over Westchester County brought their sports cars down into the business section of Mount Vernon and drag-raced around town. They took to the streets, and fighting, and before long there would be all kinds of chaos going on. Many of these kids came from homes where their parents were professional people — doctors, lawyers, school teachers, city administrators. The thing that puzzled the people who worked with the young people in Mount Vernon was exactly the reason these kids came to town and rumbled around like that — and why only on Thursday nights? Why didn't they come on Monday night, or Tuesday night, or Wednesday night, or Friday night? Why just Thursday night?

So I took to the streets with a group of the social workers, a member of the youth squad of the police department. About 6:30 in the evening we walked through the streets and, sure enough, about a quarter to seven they all came into town. The place came alive with activity. Young people were running all over the place. About fifteen minutes later, I turned to one of the responsible people and said, "I've got your answer."

He said, "You're kidding. We've been wrestling with this

problem for more than two years and you've got the answer in fifteen minutes."

I said, "Yes."

We went back to the place where we had met. I asked him to take out of the files the name of any particular boy who had been giving them real trouble from one of these upper-middleclass homes. Next, I told him to call his home and ask to speak to the maid.

He shook his head. "To the maid?"

"Yes."

So he dialed. The boy's mother answered the phone. He said, "Mrs. Waters, may I speak to the maid please?"

Mrs. Waters said, "I'm sorry, but she's not home. She won't be back until tomorrow." And she hung up.

The youth worker turned to me and said, "What does that prove?"

I said, "Very simple. These kid's parents are so busy with their social activities, that they don't have time to raise, discipline, or give affection to their kids. The *maid* is the one who does it. The maid disciplines the kids; she is the one who sees that they do their homework; sees that they get to bed on time. The maid sees that they get up in the morning; she is the one they run to when they have problems; she is the one whose shoulder they cry upon. In other words, she becomes a mother to these kids. And everybody in Westchester County knows that Thursday night is the maid's night off. So, on Thursday night — because the maid isn't home and they're unable to discipline these kids — these parents have no control over the kids at all. So you see, human nature is the same, no matter on what social level it exists."

And perhaps it might be wise to extend a word to parents here. It makes no difference how much you raise your children to be conformed to the rules and regulations of a particular society. You may raise your youngster to be the most disciplined, the most cultured, the most refined, the most respected one in the neighborhood. You can give him the latest copy of Emily Post. You may teach him when to enter a room; how to sit down; when to rise; how to seat himself at a dinner table. You may instruct him on how to pick the chicken from the bone without touching it with his fingers — to go through all the rules and regulations of being conformed to the culture of·a particular community to which you want him to belong, but the Bible declares that at your best, all of your righteousness is as filthy rags in the sight of God.

The Apostle Paul writes in Romans 7, "I know that in me, that in my flesh, dwelleth no good thing." It makes no difference how well respected, trained, and educated your child is, as long as he is detached from the Person of Jesus Christ, he is capable of any crime in the book.

You see, my parents were no different. After all, what reason did they have to believe that I was anything other than what I said? President of the young people's department in the church, president of the student body at school, getting good marks, well respected. Whenever a teacher wanted to reprimand another student for his lack of academic aggressiveness, she would say, "Why can't you be like that fellow Tom Skinner?"

I was excited by the double life that I was leading — rumbling with the guys on Saturday night, breaking in, stealing, looting, rioting, and then getting up in the young people's choir on Sunday morning and singing, "All Hail the Power of Jesus' Name."

6

A Visit to a Negro Church

At seven years of age, I joined the church because it was the respectable thing to do.

I attended basically to maintain my father's respectability as a preacher and to maintain a good front for my role as a gang leader. I'd sit in church Sunday after Sunday amused about what was going on.

Like so many other churches across America, in my church there was no real worship. Sunday morning was a time for the people to gather and be stirred by the emotional clichés that always did the trick. So long as the service was liberally sprinkled with those time-worn phrases, the people felt good. They were secure in hearing the words and acting out the roles expected. To change the order of service or the language was to tamper with the faith.

These churches are merely refilling stations for those whose spiritual lives run on the clichés, the sameness. Nothing important is ever said. Words come before thought. Songs come without any apparent reason except to rekindle that emotional spark. If the minister is soft-voiced, the congregation sleeps. If he is lively, they pay attention.

For me, as a teenager, these services had no meaning whatsoever — except as entertainment. And I've talked with hundreds of other teens who put up with this same kind of activity, Sunday after Sunday.

You get so you can predict every word and gesture of the pastor, people and choir.

In our church it was this way: At eleven o'clock, the choir came marching down the aisle dressed in their robes, singing "We're Marching to Zion," and filed into the choir loft behind the pulpit. The pastor stood up to pray. Then there was a Scripture reading; then a responsive reading from the back of the hymnal. After that, the pastor called on one of the deacons to pray. It was always one of three or four who went through the same prayer every Sunday. It went something like this: "God of our Fathers, Abraham, Isaac, and Jacob. We thank You for our lying down last night and our uprising this morning. We thank You that we're still in the land of the living and that the blood is still running warm in our veins; that we've got the activities of our limbs and the articulation of our speech. We thank You that our bed last night was not our cooling board and that our blanket was not our winding sheet. We thank You this morning that we've been able to push our way out to the house of prayer and we pray Lord that while You're moving this morning that You'll just stop by here. We pray that You'll go up to the choir, Lord, and give us that love that runs from heart to heart and breast to breast. We pray for the pastor this morning. We ask that You will prop him up on every weak and leaning side."

Meanwhile, while he was praying, some sister or brother was beginning to moan a little bit, others to hum a little. Someone interjected, "Now go on and pray that prayer, Brother." The deacon continued, "Now, Lord, we want You this morning to bless the sick and the afflicted, the poor and the needy, the prison-bound." He always closed his prayer by saying, "Now Lord, when we come down to press a dying pillar, when we've done all that You've assigned our hands and hearts to do, we want You to lead us down by chilly Jordan and let us cross over at a calm time. Take us over there to that land where Job declared that the wicked would cease from troubling and the weary could be at rest. Where every day would be Sunday afterwhile."

Then, someone picked up the word "afterwhile" and carried it out, "Afterwhile, afterwhile, afterwhile," then someone else. Before long, ten or fifteen people were saying "afterwhile." Finally, half the church, with jumping and shouting, was repeating it until no one could hear the deacon praying. Soon people were shouting all over the place. After awhile they calmed down a little bit as the choir began to pick up the chant and then sing "Sweet Hour of Prayer."

"Sweet hour of prayer, sweet hour of prayer . . . that calls me from a world of care."

The choir then began to hum. Someone jumped up and said, "That was my mother's song." Someone else would say, "Well, my father sang that song." And before long emotionalism would break loose again.

When things quieted down, the church clerk came up to read the announcements and notices for the Sunday. The pastor then spent about half an hour talking about the need for money and finances in the church. The deacons and ushers would take up two or three offerings; then the choir sang another song and the preacher was ready to preach.

Perhaps at one time it all had meaning. Perhaps the old words, the same songs, the tattered prayers still said something to some of the people. But I was not helped. The traditions, clichés and dullness only drove me further from God.

Now we were at the climax of the Sunday morning service — the sermon.

It was the usual procedure. The preacher came into the pulpit with his notebook. The night before he had pulled out a couple of books — like the sermons of Ironside or Robert E. Lee. He had copied the sermons in his notebook. Now he would walk up into the pulpit and preach them. And while he preached, the people just sat calmly as he read off his sermon. They knew he was reading a sermon. The language was stilted and the words weren't his own. The illustrations and points were from another generation. Today was no different. The preacher read — then about a half hour later, he closed his notebook. As soon as the book was closed, some sister nudged another one sitting next to her and said, "The book is closed." That meant it was now time to get ready. Another person woke up and noticed that the book was closed. Then the preacher put the book aside and shouted something like this: "I've been talking about Jesus, my rock, my sword, my shield, my wheel in the middle of a wheel."

And then he talked about how he met Jesus down in the clay hills of Georgia and how one Friday in May in a little country church, he "saw the light."

By now, the rest of the congregation was awake. A chorus of "amen's" from the people punctuated his little soliloquy. By now we had all heard it so many times we could repeat it with him — dramatic pauses, shouts and all.

At the peak of emotion, the preacher walked over to the mourner's bench, beginning another well-worn invitational sermon. After exhausting his file of cliches and illustrations, he pulled them out again. The words were designed to strike home to the hearts of the people. After fifteen minutes of the preacher's urging, the congregation responded just the way he wanted them to. They knew if they did, they could shorten the service, because the preacher expected them to moan, shout, cry and carry on. When enough people were so "moved," the preacher extended his invitation — or took another offering.

His invitation was not for seeking sinners to find salvation through the merits of Jesus Christ, but a general invitation for everyone not belonging to the church to come to the front and join.

Yes, Sunday after Sunday, it was the same.

And I was sitting there amused because I could predict almost to the minute what would happen, when it would happen, and how it would happen. It got to be a game — I could predict every Sunday morning what sister was going to get up and shout, what deacon was going to pray and what his words would be. Some of us, as young people, sat in the choir giggling and laughing as we would recite the prayer with him.

To us it became a big joke because the same deacon who prayed that long-winded, pious prayer was also a known drunk in the community. The same sister who jumped up and shouted "amen" on Sunday morning had had three husbands and was living with still another.

So the whole thing became sort of an amusing little program for us. And I was excited by the fact that I could go to church and live under the nose of the preacher and still operate as gang leader.

We all quoted the right verses and recited the right phrases in church on Sunday morning, but on Monday we faced the world with the feeling that God was unnecessary — that He didn't exist.

We — the "enlightened ones" — saw God as an emotional crutch of the people — just another word in their catalogue of clichés.

I was more convinced than ever that if this was the church, I didn't want any part of it.

7

Meeting the Negro Minister

I was bitter because the church was a meeting place for a lot of empty, emotionally-oriented people who gathered to hear the same old words and phrases that triggered the response everyone came to see and to get.

And if the churches left something to be desired, so did the preachers. I was a P.K. — a preacher's kid — and knew many ministers. And I can't recall *any* of these ministers who were really in their positions because God had chosen them to minister to the people. More often it was the people who were there to support the pastor. I can recall many conversations on the part of Negro preachers with whom I'd come in contact. For instance, one Monday a pastor said to my father, "Boy, I really preached yesterday morning. I had them niggers jumpin' benches and hollering and screaming at every word I said. And you know that I *must* have preached — because they raised $300.00 for me."

I soon became aware that Christianity was considered successful only in terms of how much money the church raised, how successful the pastor was, how big the car he drove, how good the clothing he wore, and how many competed against one another to build the largest and the biggest and the most famous church.

Through these associations with the Negro preachers of Harlem, I became aware of a tremendous number who were involved in serious sex sins. They had extra-marital affairs, committed adultery with members of their congregations and had plenty of "girl friends" when they travelled to conventions.

I was even disgusted to learn of many Harlem preachers who were involved in homosexual affairs.

The congregations winked at the sexual misbehavior of their ministers because this gave *them* license to do the same.

I soon became aware of the viciousness, hate and greed that existed among so many of the Negro clergy in the city of New York.

The churches would take three or four offerings a Sunday for various causes of one sort or another. And it was this kind of thing that turned my stomach. At least one of these offerings was for the preacher.

In many Negro communities, as I observed them as a teenager, the Negro pastor was pretty well off. For instance, there is one pastor in Harlem whose salary is $200.00 a week. And that's an adequate salary, since $200.00 a week is what a Junior Executive gets in a pretty well run organization. But then think of the fact that he lives rent-free in the church's parsonage, that most of his utilities are paid for — telephone, gas and electric. On top of all this, he is given a car every other year by the church, which usually takes care of putting the gas in the car. Then consider that the church raises anywhere from $750.00 to $1500.00 every year to send him on a four-week vacation, plus paying all his expenses to denominational conventions once a year. Finally, consider the fact that every year the church celebrates the pastor's anniversary in which every member is required to give $1.00 for every year he has been pastor. This particular pastor that I've just mentioned celebrated his fifteenth anniversary last year and one thousand people gave $1 for every year he had been pastor — $15,000! These gifts every year aren't bad fringe benefits in addition to the $200.00 a week basic salary he gets!

And so many of them exploit their people, doing what they call "milking the people dry." "Make them give," "make them honor you" is the word. Make no mention of Jesus Christ, no mention of the need to reach the down and out; no mention of the drug addicts, the alcoholic, the gang leader. No mention of mothers who are raising children on welfare checks, living in a two-by-four flat somewhere with five, six, or seven children — with only two rooms and no husband. No mention of how the church can become relevant to this situation. And I said to myself, if this is Christianity, then I want no part of it.

But many of the people weren't interested in spiritual help anyway. The church formed the only basis for social action or social security for the Negro. It was the only place that gave him a sense of status, a sense of belonging.

In society he was a nobody; in society he was looked down upon; in society he was rejected. But in the church he could become a member of any one of the thirty or forty clubs and organizations such as the Floral Club, the Pastor's Aid Club, the North Carolina Club, the Fidelis Club — and some thirty others. And for every club and organization you need a president, a vice-president, a secretary, and a treasurer. In addition, there was a corresponding secretary, assistant corresponding secretary, assistant treasurer, chaplain, and assistant chaplain. The clubs gave everyone a position. For the first time, a man who was a "nobody" in society had a title in the church. And the Negro pastor, well-schooled in what some Negro preachers called Negro psychology, who wanted to exploit this situation, used it to his advantage.

The pastors would have what was called a Pastor's Aid Club. The purpose of that organization, of course, was to aid the pastor. Once a month they put on special programs in which money was raised to aid the pastor, to help buy his new car, to furnish a new apartment just above the church, to buy him two or three new suits. This, of course, was in addition to his salary.

In a typical Negro Baptist Church, the way you join the church is very simple. The preacher preaches a message on Sunday morning and gets the people emotionally worked up.

When he finishes, the choir sings. Then the preacher does what they call "opening the doors of the church." The pastor stands and says, "Now if anybody wants to come by letter as a candidate for baptism, or on Christian experience, you get up out of your seat and walk down the aisle." After you come forward and the singing is all over, a church clerk stands up and reads your name and address and says, "We have with us this morning Master Thomas Skinner who resides at 269 - 153rd Street, New York City, and desires to become a member of Daystar Baptist Church as a candidate for baptism." And the pastor says, "You've heard the recommendation come from the church clerk. What is your pleasure?" A deacon then stands and says, "I make a motion that Master Thomas Skinner becomes a member of Daystar Baptist Church after having been immersed in the water."

Someone else says, "I second the motion."

Pastor says, "It's been properly moved and seconded that Master Thomas Skinner becomes a member of Daystar Baptist Church upon being immersed in the water. What is your pleasure? All in favor say, aye."

All the people say "aye."

"Are there any nays?" No one opposes. Soon they shake your hand and welcome you to the church and tell you, "Brother Skinner, if you'll come back on the second Sunday in December we'll baptize you. Meanwhile, stop over at the table and pick up your due envelopes and pay your dues every Sunday."

That's all there was to it. To practically every pastor, a person walking down the aisle was just another dollar sign. He never saw another human soul thirsty to know God.

Once again I resolved that if this was Christianity, I wanted no part of it. To me it was made up of phonies, hypocrites, actors, and money-makers who were in the business solely for what they could get out of it and who were not the least bit interested in the souls of men.

8

What Made the Difference

Yes, I was sick and tired of religion. The only reason I went to church, as already mentioned, was to keep up my front — preacher's kid, but leader of the tough Harlem Lords.

I led the fellows in more than fifteen large scale gang fights and we never lost. The name Harlem Lords became a name respected and feared throughout the Harlem community.

I had only one ambition — that my gang would become *the gang* in Harlem. I had 129 fellows in the gang, every one of them eating out of my hand. If I told a fellow to go home and steal from his own mother, he'd do it. Excited by the thrill and the opportunity of having so much power, I became more and more bigoted every day.

Finally, I got to the place where I hated all whites. I hated the ground they stood on. Anyone who didn't belong to my race made me boil up in anger. I had no other reason than the obvious ones. I just couldn't stand white people.

I began to blame white society for the total dilemma that the Negro faced. More and more I took this frustration out in the things we did.

One night I was preparing strategy for a gang fight. This would be no normal gang fight. It would be the largest gang rumble ever to take place in the city of New York. It would involve five gangs — the Lords, the Imperials, the Crowns, the Sportsmen, and the Jesters.

These gangs were going to unite together to fight a coalition of gangs from the other side of the city.

This gang rumble would involve more than 3,000 fellows on the street at one time! It amounted to a small war! My job — to plan the strategy. I had done it many times before. I had led the fellows in gang fights where the gangs numbered three and four times as many as we were. Sometimes 130 of us would take on gangs of 250 or 300 fellows. I knew how to map out the strategy. Part of the skill that kept me leader of the Harlem Lords for over two years was this ability to plan every situation.

On this particular night I had my radio on, listening to my favorite disc jockey. It was a rock and roll program that came on every night between the hours of eight and ten o'clock.

The frantic beat of the music throbbed and filled the small room where I was working. Laying out plans for attacks, counter-attacks, diversionary maneuvers and tactics to employ when the police were called, I chuckled to myself. What can the entire New York police department do to stop a rumble involving 3,000 guys?

I reached for another piece of paper on which to scribble ideas and tactics. I glanced at my watch — nine o'clock. Normally, at nine o'clock there was a station break, a commercial, and the disc jockey returned to the air with the rest of the program. But on this particular night, instead of the disc jockey returning with the regular program after the commercial was over, an unscheduled gospel program came on.

Now I was highly irritated, to say the least. I had had my fill of religion. I'd gotten enough of that from my father and many of the Harlem churches.

I swore softly and banged my fist in my hand. The other thing that annoyed me was the fact that the radio preacher was the most uncouth, uneducated one I'd ever listened to. He split his infinitives, he got his adjectives mixed up with his verbs. He sounded as though he hadn't gone to school a day in his life. And I felt that if a preacher was dumb enough to believe in God, at least he could sound intelligent about it.

The third thing that bothered me was the fact that the preacher was emotional. He was the kind of preacher who became a little excited about God, about Jesus Christ, about religion, and I felt that if a person had to believe all that business about God and Christ and sin and death and hell and heaven, at least he could keep quiet about his feelings.

I tried to turn to another station. But somehow I found myself compelled to listen to this uncouth preacher.

I went on mapping out the strategy that I planned, trying to ignore what the preacher was saying. Yet, what he was saying got through to me.

This uncouth, uneducated preacher spoke from II Corinthians, chapter 5, verse 17, a passage which says, "Wherefore, if any man be in Christ he is a new creature. Old things are passed away and behold all things are become new."

I had heard that Scripture passage a hundred times if I heard it once. But never the way he explained it. "It doesn't matter who you are, where you come from, or what you have done, because Christ came to earth for the purpose of taking upon Himself every sin you have ever committed." And he said I had a sinful nature and described it as a factory inside man which manufactures evil and causes a man to commit sin. He said, "It's not the fact that a person is a drunkard, or an alcoholic, or a drug addict, or an adulterer, or a thief, or a cheat, or a liar that makes him immoral. No! That man is born with a condition in his human nature — a factory inside him that causes him to act contrary to God. That old sinful nature causes a man to do the things he does." He quoted a passage of Scripture in the seventh chapter of Romans where the Apostle Paul says, "I know that in me, that is in my flesh, dwelleth no good thing."

I put down the papers I was working on, lost in a new train of thought. Somehow I got the spooky feeling this guy was talking right to me.

"No, it's not the fact that you commit sin that makes you a sinner. You're a sinner — that's why you commit sin." His uneducated delivery was also uncomplicated. The picture he painted was very clear to me.

He continued as I listened.

"Jesus Christ is your answer. He's the only One who can straighten the whole mess out. He gets right to the root of the problem. He changes that 'factory' inside you that makes you sin. Yessir! That's what He does!"

I was no longer conscious of any emotionalism. The man went on. "When Jesus was nailed to that cross, your sin was nailed there to that cross with Him. He died to pay for every sin you ever committed or ever will commit. And He rose again to live His life inside you. That's right! His Spirit lives in that 'factory' and makes it over so you don't sin no more."

For the first time in my life I took a good look at Tom Skinner. Not so much what Tom Skinner had *done* — the money I'd stolen, the fact that there were fellows who were going to bear permanent bodily injury for the rest of their lives because of me and the gang fights I'd led. But I began to think of what I had *become* — arrogant, proud, bigoted, hateful. I was as bigoted as any white racist. And yet, here was a man saying that Jesus Christ was prepared to change all of that.

"That's right! The Lord Jesus can make it possible for you to stand in the very presence of God Himself — just as if you had never sinned."

I had never really heard this message before. My only contact with religion had been the distorted, phony brand of Christianity from my earlier days. Now here a man was telling me that God would forgive every sin I had ever committed and then make me a new person — make it possible for me to stand in the presence of God just as if I had never sinned.

It all sounded good, except for a couple of problems.

Problem number one was that everything that preacher said that night he quoted from the Bible. And my opinion about the Bible was that it was a nice poetic religious history book that had some nice religious poetry in it about dealings of some sort of Supreme Being with a bunch of superstitious people who had the audacity to believe that He existed.

I further argued that I didn't understand God and I said, "Why should I commit myself to a God I don't understand, that I cannot logically figure out? Why should I commit myself to a God who doesn't make sense to my human mind?" I considered myself a philosophical realist and as a realist I said, "If you want me to believe God, then I've got to touch Him. I've got to see Him. I've got to feel Him. I'm not going to commit myself to something I can't see, touch, or feel."

Even though I was a gang leader, I considered myself a teenage intellectual. By the time I was fourteen I could tell you the difference between existentialism and rationalism; between Freudian's psychology and behavioristic psychology. I was acquainted with the works of such men as Jean Paul Sartre and existentialism. I was well read in Bertrand Russell, that great philosophical agnostic. And I knew the writings of other great philosophers like Socrates, Plato, Aristotle, Francis Bacon, Spencer.

I reasoned that since I could read these men and grasp some of the great philosophical teachings that had been handed down through humanity, then for what, in all the world, did I need Jesus Christ? I could stand on my own two feet, think for myself. One of my favorite poems was

> It matters not how strait the gate,
> How charged with punishments the scroll;
> I am the master of my fate;
> I am the captain of my soul.

I believed it — that I was the master of my own soul. I could determine my own destiny. I thought I had the intellectual ability to stand on my own two feet. As far as I was concerned, God was for emotionally disturbed people who needed that kind of a crutch, for Sunday school kids who didn't know any better, for older people who were about to die and needed some sort of hope to cling to. But Tom Skinner could think for himself.

But one by one, that night, my arguments began to be smashed. I argued that I couldn't see God, couldn't touch Him, couldn't feel Him. But my mind flashed back to my science class that day when the science teacher began to lecture by saying, "Today we're going to study the atom — a-t-o-m." He said, "The atom cannot be seen by the human eye. It cannot be seen under a normal microscope. It cannot be seen even under some of the most powerful electro-microscopes." As teacher of the class, he admitted that he had never seen an atom. Then he said that this atom, which he had never seen, was divided into three parts — a proton, neutron, and electron. Now wasn't that ridiculous? He had never seen an atom, didn't know what it looked like, but he did know that it had three parts to it. And he expected *me* to believe it. Yet, I did believe it and in fact, I still do. I believe in nuclear fission, atomic energy. I believe in atomic explosions and nuclear power. All of these things are structured upon the fact that the atom does exist and although we don't know what an atom or a proton looks like, we believe in the atomic bomb. Well, the evidence for God is much more conclusive. Why can't I accept the fact that God exists even though I can't see Him?

You know, your own mind and conscience will sometimes tell you more than you think. I'm sure we *know* a lot more than we'd like to admit. There are things we *don't want to believe*. Such was the case with me.

This uneducated radio speaker wasn't really changing any of my suppositions. I was doing it *myself*. I was seeing the weaknesses of my own logic. Just as in the case of the atom, there are things that exist and take place constantly, every day. We know they're there, even though we can't see them or *prove* their existence.

Any person who looks at the precision and the symmetry and the beauty of this universe and draws the conclusion that it "just came about" is crazy. What if I should put a beautiful watch in front of you, one of the best precision

21-jewel watches ever made — a watch so precise it is accurate to one one-thousandth of a second every year, put together with the finest craftsmanship and workmanship? And when you ask me where I got it I tell you it "just happened to come about; conditions were right for it to be there." You'd think I was mentally deranged! You would say, "Tom, it's ridiculous because anyone can see that this watch with its precision was put together by a superior intelligence. It just didn't happen."

Yet, I had been looking at this universe with its tremendous laws, its thousands upon thousands of planets and stars hurtling through space at fantastic speeds and never colliding, and I had said it "just came about."

I began to realize that there were many things in my everyday life that I accepted, believed or trusted that I could not see. They taught me in biology that there was vitamin A in carrots, vitamin B in rice, vitamin C in orange juice, vitamin D in milk. To this day I don't know what vitamin D looks like, but I drink milk and I love it. There were other things in my everyday life that I believed and accepted that I could not see, touch, or feel. *Why not God?* I asked myself.

But I argued that the Bible was written by men and since the men who wrote it were human, the Bible was subject to human error. But it suddenly hit me that I was also a student of history. Everything I learned about history I learned from a history book and they taught me in history books and in history class that Julius Caesar conquered Pompey in 44 B.C. They taught me that Marcus Aurelius ruled Rome in A.D. 280. They taught me that the Declaration of Independence was signed in 1776. And they taught me that the French Revolution broke out in 1789. In addition, they gave me a lot of other facts and dates. I believed them simply because my history book said so. And who wrote my history book? A man. Yet when it came to the Bible, written over a period of 1600 years by more than forty different authors, from different backgrounds, without prior collaboration and *without contradiction,* I didn't want to believe it.

One of my favorite arguments against Jesus was, how do we *know* He really existed? How do we know that accounts of Jesus aren't some carefully preserved legend? Then I recalled one of my favorite characters of history. Socrates was a Greek philosopher and the only proof that we have that Socrates ever lived, is what Plato says about him. Only *one person* wrote about Socrates. Except for a Greek play writer by the name of Aristophanes who depicts Socrates in one of his comical plays, Plato is the only authority that we have in all of history that Socrates ever lived! And yet we accept his story. And yet more than forty different men sat down and wrote about the greatness and the sovereignty and the power of God, and when many men — writing separately — gave similar and non-contradictory accounts of Jesus Christ — I didn't believe it.

I never met Julius Caesar. I didn't see Julius Caesar conquer Pompey. I wasn't around when the Declaration of Independence was signed; I never met George Washington; I never met others of the great historical characters. I can't prove to you that there ever was a battle called the Battle of Waterloo where Napoleon Bonaparte and his armies were defeated. But I accept what my history book says. I began to realize these intellectual arguments stood on very shaky ground.

My arguments were being shot down — by my own reason and examination. My last resort was the argument that I didn't understand God or how He could exist or work. I felt I had to know more about Him before I could believe.

But, again, came an answer to my argument.

I argued that I didn't understand God. But neither did I understand the national monetary system, or the balance of payments between nations, or the gold reserve system. I didn't understand a lot of the economic factors that controlled the stock market, that created an "up market" and a "down market" — a bear market and a bull market. And I didn't know all of the intricate processes that make the

Federal reserve board work and how easing credit benefits some people and is a disadvantage to others. I didn't know all of the intricate processes behind economics. Yet, though I didn't understand what makes the stock market work — though I didn't understand all the general processes behind this international monetary system, we're supposed to live under — I was certainly not going to stop spending money until I found out.

A survey shows that the average person who drives an automobile does not know all of the intricate processes that go on inside that car to make it go. For a great many people, all they know is that you get in the car, put the ignition key in, turn it, step on the pedal, and take off, and that you turn the steering wheel at certain times. But they don't know what makes an automobile tick. Yet, they have faith in it. They don't understand it, but they trust it. Though they don't completely understand all the processes inside, they drive it.

And yet when it came to God, I argued that I must understand Him. Suddenly I began to realize that God wasn't asking me to understand everything, but He was asking me to believe the evidence that I *did* have.

The evidence was that Tom Skinner was a phony and that Jesus Christ died for phonies. The radio speaker had shown me that Tom Skinner, with his bigotry, hate and violence, could never — through his own strength and energy — be able to produce anything in life that would be worthwhile. He told me that Jesus Christ died in my place, to forgive me of every sin that I'd ever committed, and arose again to live in me. And God was asking me to believe just that.

I began to consider the fact that I had never done what every true intellectual is supposed to do. He must never draw conclusions about that with which he has never really experimented. Every scientist knows you must never draw conclusions about anything you have never put to the test.

I had never really put Jesus Christ to the test, never really given Him an opportunity to work in my life. I had never given Him a chance to come inside and live in me and prove whether the things the Bible said about Him were really true.

As a student of science I was a strong believer in the scientific method. The scientific method taught me that you must find out what you want to prove, then get all the information that you can get about that particular subject. Once you've accumulated all the data, the next step is to classify that information, then put it in some sort of logical order. Next, based on the classification of that information and some sort of logical order, you venture what science calls a guess or a theory. But once you come up with a theory, that is not enough. Every true scientist knows that beyond the theoretical stage, if theory is to become law or fact, you must experiment and prove over and over that something happens.

It occurred to me that I had never really put God to the test, that I had never taken Him beyond the theoretical test. I had just drawn intellectual and philosophical conclusions about God, but had never given Him a chance to work in my life.

I bowed my head and prayed simply, "God . . . I don't understand all of this. I don't understand how You're going to change my life. I don't even understand why I'm praying to You, but if these things are true . . . if what this preacher says is true . . . if what the Bible really says is true . . . if You *can* transform my life and make me a new person . . . if You can forgive me of every sin that I have ever committed, then I'm asking You to do it. I'm asking You to come into my life and take it over and live in me."

No trumpets. No shouts. No visions. But He did just that. I *knew* Jesus Christ came into my life in answer to that prayer.

There were no blinding flashes of light, no mountains caved in, no thunder roared. There was no emotional, traumatic experience that night. I simply accepted God at His Word. You see, once you accept the existence of God, God can only be God by virtue of the fact that He doesn't lie.

Whatever He does is never less than perfect, and if everything God says is perfect, then the words of Jesus Christ when He says, "Him that cometh unto me I will in no wise cast out," are also perfect. And that particular night I came to Jesus Christ. Because God can't lie, Jesus Christ actually took up residence in my life and began to live in me, and He's been living there ever since.

It's been the most thrilling, the most adventurous life I believe a person could ever live. I've had the privilege of actually having the God of heaven and earth live inside me. I've had the privilege of living in that close, personal relationship with Jesus Christ.

I turned the radio off and began to think about the wonder of this new life — and was confronted with a reminder of the old Tom Skinner.

There in front of me were the plans for the rumble. Here was a dilemma!

9

Launching the New Life

Y ou don't just walk up to a gang of fel-
lows that you've been leading around for two years in rioting, looting, fighting and lawbreaking and say, "Well, guys,
it's been nice knowing you. So long."

No one quits a gang. In fact, just two weeks before I
had personally broken the arms and legs of two fellows who
told me *they* were going to quit. And these fellows got off
easy.

There were only two guys who ever successfully quit the
gang and got away with it. And that was only because
their parents called the police and they were given an
around-the-clock police guard while they and their parents
packed up and left town.

It was impossible to quit the gang and walk around the
same neighborhood healthy. But I recalled the radio broadcast I heard the night before.

The preacher signed off the air that night by saying that
the promise of God to any person who receives Christ is that
He will never leave you nor forsake you. He quoted a passage from the Bible that went like this: "Jesus says, Lo I
am with you alway, even unto the end of the world."

That's all I had to protect myself as I walked to the meeting place of the Harlem Lords — just a promise of God.

I moved into the smoky room and walked to the front.
There were 129 fellows in that room. Every one of them

carried a knife. Some had guns — and none of them had any reservations about using their weapons. Yet, I knew what had to be done. I had to tell the gang what happened to me the night before and why I was quitting the Harlem Lords. "Man, you're a fool, 'cause you won't get out of here alive," I told myself.

The voices quieted down and I could feel all eyes on me. They were expecting a briefing for the big, all-out rumble. I prayed silently. "God, if I ever needed You, it's now."

I motioned for silence and began to speak. I told of the broadcast — how the speaker had given me insight to truth I'd never heard before. I told them that I was convinced Jesus Christ had died for all the sins I'd ever committed, and had given me everlasting life.

"Last night, I asked Him to come inside me and live in me. And He answered me," I said.

All the time I was talking, I could see the number two man in the gang. His nickname was "The Mop." We called him "The Mop" because whenever there was a gang fight, this fellow wasn't happy unless he drew blood from someone and wiped his foot in it. I knew "The Mop" wanted to be number one man. He would term my telling them that I had committed my life to Jesus Christ as a sign of weakness. And he would relish the opportunity to put his knife between my ribs or across my throat.

I forced myself to finish without weakening.

"I don't understand everything involved, but I know that Christ has taken up residence in my life. And based on that commitment, I can no longer responsibly lead the gang."

You could have heard a pin drop. No one spoke. No one even moved. I walked down the aisle and out into the night air, half expecting a knife to come tearing into my back or a bullet to dig into my flesh. But nothing! I walked out without one person raising a hand against me.

I nearly shouted my thankfulness to God.

Two nights later I saw "The Mop" on the street. He motioned to me and said, "Tom, I wanna talk to you."

We stopped and he grinned. "You know," he said, "the other night when you got up and walked out of that meeting I was gonna really cut you up. I was all set to put my knife right in your back."

"And why didn't you?"

"I couldn't move," he said, his eyes growing wider. "It was like somebody was holding me back — like I was glued to my seat!"

He licked his lips and continued. "And I talked to some of the other guys, too. I wasn't the only one. They said the same thing — that something, or somebody, actually held them back in their seats."

Now my eyes widened and I felt the hair on the back of my neck rise.

"What d'ya make of it, Tom?" he asked.

"I know that the Christ I've committed myself to isn't just some fictitious character who lived two thousand years ago . . . some nebulous spirit floating around in the air somewhere. I know now that Jesus Christ is alive! He's real! What David said of Him was true, 'Even though I walk through the valley of the shadow of death I will fear no evil for thou art with me,' " I said.

The toughness was gone from my former associate in crime. I turned to "The Mop" and asked, "Would you like to know who that 'Somebody' was who kept you glued to your seat?"

He nodded.

Standing on 153rd Street and McCombs Place — two blocks from the Polo Grounds — an ex-gang leader, a Christian less than 48 hours, led another gang member to Christ. Apart from the thrill of my own commitment to Christ, I can't think of any other experience as thrilling as introducing "The Mop" to Jesus Christ.

"The Mop" has since graduated from law school and has entered one of the largest law firms in the city of New York, proof that Jesus Christ transforms the whole individual.

If you want to change a man, you must change *him*. You can't change a man by changing his environment, by removing his circumstances. You can't change a man simply by trying to build a new type of community for him.

You see, society is made up of people. If you want to change society, you have to change people, and the only person who can change another person is Jesus Christ. Second Corinthians 5:17 is true. If any man is "in Christ" he *is* a new creature.

If I had not been reached by Jesus Christ I would either be dead, in prison, or graduated to a higher form of hoodlumism. Without my conversion, I could be a drug addict standing on 116th Street scratching my head waiting for the next pusher to come along, or I might be one of those running around the country helping to create riots. I was already being trained for it.

But at this very moment, I'm a new person. Every sin I have ever committed has been completely forgiven. Jesus Christ is alive in me. My life has new meaning and purpose because of Him.

The tremendous work that the Spirit of God had done in my life in transforming me soon became evident to me. He took the bigotry, hate and violence out of my life. I had reached the place where I hated white people and blamed them for all the atrocities, immorality and social injustices that were brought against the Negro. Now that hate was gone.

In a football game several weeks later, my new-found Christian love met another test. I played left guard on the team. It was my job on end runs or off tackle plays to run interference when the halfback took the ball. So when the quarterback called an end run play, I pulled out and blocked the defensive end, knocking him out of play. The halfback went through and scored.

We were getting up from the ground to head back to the huddle for the point after touchdown. The kid that I happened to block got up and was furious. He jumped in front of me and slammed me in the stomach. As I bent over from the blow he hacked me across the back. I hit the ground as he kicked me, shouting, "You dirty black nigger! I'll teach you a thing or two!"

Under normal circumstances the old Tom Skinner would have jumped up and pulverized this white boy. But instead, I got up from the ground and found myself looking this fellow in the face. A smile broke across my face and I said to him, "You know, because of Jesus Christ, I love you anyway."

You know, I surprised *myself*. But what the Bible said was true. I had just seen it work! If any man be in Christ he is a new creature. I *was* a new person! Here was Tom Skinner who, six weeks before, would have tried to kill this white bigot, barehanded. Now I was able to look into the face I normally would have smashed, and tell him that I loved him in Christ.

The kid threw his helmet down to the ground, ran off the field, and couldn't play for the rest of the game. When the game was over he met me in the locker room and said to me, "Tom, you've done more to knock prejudice out of me by telling me that you loved me than you would have if you'd socked my jaw in."

I became convinced that the only answer to the prejudice, the bigotry, and the hate that exists in our world today is that people allow the love of God through the Person of Jesus Christ to be expressed through them. Love does not come naturally. Love is not part of human nature. It is not in the nature and desire of man to love instead of to hate. That type of life can only be produced by the Person of Jesus Christ.

10

Going Out With the Message

The streets of Harlem are always crowded. Except when the weather is really bad, there are sometimes hundreds of people just standing on the corners.

There is the derelict, without work, without money, without hope of ever having dignity.

There are the thousands of drug addicts — some 60,000 in Harlem — pacing nervously while waiting for a "pusher" to come by to give them another "fix." Some of the addicts are looking for things to steal to pay for their next shot.

Prostitutes try to "hustle" customers to pay for their drugs — or the drugs of husbands.

And when school is out, the kids are on the streets. They roam from early morning until sometimes after midnight. The eight-to-ten-year olds are forming sub-gangs.

After my conversion, these people became my concern. I became deeply concerned about thousands of other fellows like Tom Skinner who needed to hear the truth about this person Jesus Christ. They needed someone on their own level, someone who understood their language, someone who understood the anguish, suffering, and frustration that develop when a kid is born and raised in a community like Harlem. I know the bitterness of the kid who feels trapped — who feels there is no opportunity, no way out for him. If he can hear the truth about Jesus Christ, it can be the most liberating force in his life. For the first time he can pick up his head and really begin to live. Jesus Christ says, "I have come that they might have life, and that they might have it more abundantly."

This is the message for the people of the street, for Harlem. We didn't have to go search for them, we didn't have to look for them, we didn't have to build anything to attract them. They were there. It was just a matter of knowing how to communicate and to get the word to them that Jesus Christ cared — about them.

Following my conversion, I led several of my former gang to the Lord. I was thrilled to see my faith reproduce itself through the Holy Spirit working in the lives of the guys. But I prayed for more effective ways of reaching the thousands of kids in Harlem.

Without giving much thought to the serious implications involved, a group of us picked out certain days during the week and went out in the street to confront individuals with the claims of Jesus Christ. Sometimes we would rent portable loudspeakers and stand on the street corner and actually have large street meetings. This wasn't too difficult when you consider the fact that as many as six hundred people are within ear shot on a street corner, and sometimes maybe even a thousand. You can get a good listening audience with the many hundreds of people going back and forth.

One of my first experiences was an effort that took us down to 118th Street, around Fifth Avenue. It's a heavily populated area — an area where the gang known as the "Diablos" operated.

The "Diablo" gang was one the Lords had fought about two months before my conversion. We defeated them pretty badly. It was into this area that we went to talk about Jesus Christ.

I was standing on the corner, preaching to the crowds of teenagers who stood around or passed by. Others listened from tenement windows. While preaching, I noticed two fellows who were members of the "Diablo" gang standing

71

on the other side of the street. Within a couple of minutes, they disappeared. Soon they came back with a dozen more fellows. Before long, twenty-five, thirty, then forty fellows gathered on the other side of the street. I knew what they were thinking. "That looks like Tom Skinner." "That looks like the guy who led the Lords against us not too long ago." When the meeting on the street was finished, the crowd began to disperse.

Within a matter of moments the "Diablo" gang had converged across the street. They surrounded us and very sarcastically one of them said, "You are one of the Lords, aren't you?"

A couple of them had already pulled out their switchblades, others had bottles gripped in their hands. I knew what they had in mind.

Very calmly I said to them, "Look, fellows, before we fight out here on the street, let me tell you something. I'm not the same Tom Skinner you fought against a couple of months ago." For twenty minutes I stood there on the street and shared with them my personal testimony of how Jesus Christ had transformed my life.

"The frustration that caused me to be involved in the gang, and do the things I did, has now been settled by this Person, Jesus Christ, who is now living in me."

I challenged them with the fact that Christ could do the same thing in their lives. By the time I finished, several of these fellows actually had tears running down their cheeks. Many of them dropped their knives right on the street. Later, we counted at least fifteen switchblades that had been dropped to the ground at that invitation.

Several of the fellows came up and put their arms around us, asking how they could come to know this Person, Jesus Christ; how they could have all of their sins forgiven, how they could become new people.

And there on the street corner, we led at least twenty-five members of the "Diablo" gang to Jesus Christ. Many of them prayed openly on the street. And for a person who had just come to know Jesus Christ only a few weeks, for a person who was just now beginning to enter into a phase of witnessing about Jesus Christ to other people, this was a most thrilling moment.

We began to see results like this in many different communities and on many street corners. Day after day, we made it our business to attempt to win at least one person to Jesus Christ, to witness of the saving power and ability of this Person, Jesus Christ. And we saw fellows who were the potential top racketeers in New York City finding Jesus Christ. We saw girls who, if they were allowed to go the way they were travelling, would end up as prostitutes or drug addicts. Some of them, if they continued, would end up raising five or six children on welfare without a father. But now, because we had the opportunity of meeting them when they were in their early teens, and confronting them with the claims of Jesus Christ, their lives were being redirected.

On the weekends, we dressed up in dungarees, polo-shirts, and dirty sneakers, and picked out a target community. We went to the basketball courts in the communities where we knew a known gang was operating. There we would play on that basketball court day after day, four or five hours a day, until we got to know the leader of the guys in the neighborhood. Once we found him, we tried to win him as a friend — not to try and cram religion down his throat. You see, so many of these fellows on the street can't believe anyone really cares about them. Even in the gang it's difficult for a guy to trust someone as a friend. Most guys who belong to gangs live in constant fear, wondering who is going to turn against them, who is going to try to challenge their leadership, who is going to try to out-do them.

But once we won this fellow as a friend, we began the process of sharing with him what Jesus Christ had done in our own personal lives. And what a thrill it was to see one guy after another, one gang leader after another, one gang member after another, turning to Jesus Christ. We became tremendously excited about this ministry that God had committed to us. This business of witnessing to guys and girls at school, on street corners, in basement hideouts, recreation centers and playgrounds went on quietly.

During this time, I was also enrolled in Bible school classes at the Manhattan Bible Institute in New York City. There I was being grounded in the fundamentals of theology and Scripture.

Balancing my ministry to the street gangs was a ministry to kids *in churches*. These teenagers were in church and only going through the motions, just as I had been doing before I came to know Christ. Many of them found it difficult to understand what it meant to know — in an experience of faith — Jesus Christ. Often, I found myself coming into open conflict with some of the leading pastors within the association of Negro churches (men who were not teaching their young people about the claims of Jesus Christ).

Many of the young people, though, became very interested and invited me to their churches to discuss these issues with them. I went eagerly — and tried to challenge these young people about what it means to really know Christ, what it means to have Christ living in an individual. I told them how Christ could make it possible for us to live upright lives before God. The tragedy was that I was too *late* for many of these young people. At sixteen or seventeen, they were already well experienced in pre-marital sex, narcotics and crime. Many of the girls in these churches were dropping out of high school and subsequently church because they were pregnant. Many of them were becoming disgusted with church because of the extra-marital affairs that were going on between ministers, deacons and other leaders of the churches. These young people knew what was happening and they were looking for something real. And they weren't finding it in church.

As I began to get into their churches and speak in their youth department meetings, I began to see results. I saw teenagers responding to the claims of Jesus Christ.

Some pastors were beginning to see some real results among the young people. They invited me to conduct week-long meetings in their churches among the young people.

That is the way my preaching ministry began. And we really saw God begin to work.

11

The Young Preacher

Maybe I should say God worked in spite of those who claimed to be His children. As I began my ministry with young people in the churches of New York's Negro community, I encountered more direct opposition than I did when I preached on the street.

Many Negro clergymen resented the fact that their young people were being told that church membership alone did not guarantee them personal salvation.

Whether wisely or unwisely, I de-emphasized church membership and emphasized a personal relationship with Jesus Christ. The pastors interpreted this as rebellion against the established order of the church and accused me of trying to overthrow church authority and get the young people to leave the church.

I'm sure my age had much to do with their judgments. I was only sixteen at the time, but was being recognized more and more in Negro churches in New York City as an evangelistic preacher. Several churches that did not have pastors began to seriously consider me — even in my teens — to be pastor of their church.

Certainly, the offers were attractive. As I've already stated — the Negro minister usually does quite well financially. But more and more, I could sense the fact that God had called me as an evangelistic preacher. On June 2, 1959, when I was just turning seventeen, the United Missionary Baptist Association of Greater New York and Vicinity ordained me as a Baptist minister.

Then the heat was really put on. More and more ministers resented the fact that I placed emphasis upon the fact that man is born in sin and that there is something in man that is not like God. I preached that man cannot get rid of this spiritual problem merely by joining a church, or by becoming religious. And being young and full of zeal, I even pressed some of the ministers of the largest churches in New York City personally about *their* relationship with Jesus Christ. I challenged them as to whether Christ was running their lives and whether their ministries were really Christ-centered. I asked them if they were really interested in their people coming to know Christ and having everlasting life, or were they merely interested in building churches, raising large offerings and having the reputation of being "big preachers"?

I suppose it seemed pretty presumptuous to them to have a teenager preaching to them — and perhaps it was. But I felt that it was justified.

The personal lives of many of the Negro clergy needed attention. Many of them blatantly committed sin.

I got my chance to really speak out on this problem which so disgusted the dedicated clergymen and disillusioned the young people until they left the church.

In July, 1960, my name was placed on the program as speaker at a ministers' conference. I spent many weeks in preparation for that message, and prayed that God would give me the message He wanted me to deliver. It became clear what He wanted me to speak about. He wanted me to challenge these men from the Word of God, and I grew fearful.

I knew what it meant to go against the wishes of the minister's association. Through gossip and the use of their influence and power, they can literally ruin a young minister. I know of young preachers who started out meaning business for God but who were forced to compromise their message and morals by the association of ministers.

I knew that if I delivered the message that God was leading me to deliver, it might be the end of my ministry among these people. But I had learned a lesson the night after I had committed my life to Christ — that my Lord would not forsake me. I claimed another promise — Philippians, chapter 1, verse 6, "Being confident of this very thing, that he which hath begun a good work in you will perform it until the day of Jesus Christ."

So I stood that day before the ministers' conference in a large Harlem church, packed to capacity, and delivered the message from the Word of God entitled, "Revolution for Jesus Christ or the Status Quo?"

Right down the line, I emphasized the fact that the kind of minister Jesus Christ is calling for in the twentieth century is one who will stand uncompromisingly and speak the truth about Jesus Christ. I challenged them with the moral state of many of our ministers. I said, "As long as there is sin in our midst, we will never be able to experience the mighty movement of the Holy Spirit! Unless we clean house among ourselves, unless the clergymen of Harlem can develop the reputation of being men of God, men of holiness, men of character, truth, uprightness, we will never be able to shake the community for Jesus Christ. There are literally thousands of young people in the Harlem area who are disgusted with religion because of the immoral lives of some of their pastors!"

I challenged them to return to the Word of God. "Less and less emphasis is being placed upon sin, upon judgment, upon the death of Christ on the cross and His ability to cleanse man of sin. And more and more emphasis is placed on organization, church membership, larger offerings, higher salaries, better cars to drive and better clothes to wear. All the emphasis is being placed upon the material."

At the close of the message, I offered an invitation for every minister there who had never committed his life to Jesus Christ to do so.

I concluded with a warning; "Unless there is a change in your ministry here in Harlem — unless there is spiritual renewal, things will get worse. Your congregations will leave. Your denominations will split and there will be increased strife in this organization."

When I finished, the place was silent. No one moved. Finally, one minister got up and made this statement, "There comes a time in all of history when God has to raise up a prophet to speak the truth to us. We may not always like hearing that truth, but nevertheless, it must be said." Then he sat down.

I prayed silently that God's Spirit would work in their hearts as He had in my own. Then another minister stood. He was a most influential Negro pastor and leader in one of the larger religious organizations. He said, "Let's be honest about this thing. This young man does not know what he is talking about. After seventy-two years that our denomination has been together, this young whippersnapper stands up and predicts that we are going to split."

He became angrier as he spoke, denying the things that were said about immorality among some of the clergymen. He shook his fist at me. "Who does this youngster, only eighteen years old, think he is talking that way to respected members of the clergy three times his age?"

Another minister rose and continued the tirade. The conference broke up in angry confusion and noise. After the session had been dismissed, one minister walked up to me and said, "If you were my child, I'd take my fist right now and rap you in the jaw!"

A minister walked up behind him and cursed me with the most vulgar language any person could ever use. Another minister came up to me and said, "I feel like taking you right now and ripping you apart."

In the days to follow, I received threatening telegrams and telephone calls. Some told me I should leave the city. Others told me they'd do everything possible to see that I would never preach at another church in New York City.

I will never forget the darkness of the days that followed, as I received one threatening call after another. An association of Negro churches met the week I had preached that message, and all they could discuss during their entire session was "the message Tom Skinner preached." They were really disturbed.

After the denomination split less than three months later, a few remembered my predictions. One minister had the courage to come up and say to me, "Tom, I'm sorry. You were right."

But in spite of the concentrated opposition against me, I did continue to speak in Harlem churches. One Sunday I was the speaker in the church pastored by Adam Clayton Powell. In the evening meeting, I gave an invitation for all who really wanted to receive Jesus Christ into their lives, to come forward. More than fifty-five people got out of their seats and came to the front of the church publicly to declare their need for Jesus Christ.

Out of that church came a group of young people who became concerned about other Harlem teenagers. We formed a youth group dedicated to using every available means to reach Negro teens for Jesus Christ.

We met for several weeks, praying desperately that God would show us how we could bring the gospel message to Harlem as never before.

12

The Ripples Widen

Being young and naive has its advantages. We believed God would answer our prayers. After this group of young people had met for several weeks and had prayed much about how we could reach teenagers for Jesus Christ, we decided to venture into our first *crusade*. We decided to have it at a church located in the middle of a very populated area. In fact, directly across the street from the church was one of the largest houses of prostitution in Harlem. Just a few blocks away from the church was one of the biggest housing developments in the Harlem community. We approached the pastor of the church and asked him if we could rent the church for that week. He agreed to let us use the church for $150.00 for six nights.

That was only the beginning. We were just teenagers and people in our early twenties who put up the money out of our own pockets to sponsor the crusade.

By calling people on the telephone and by word of mouth on the street, we advertised our meetings.

We began the crusade that summer on a Monday night in August and carried it through until Saturday night. It was tremendous to see that church literally packed every night. By the end of the week, we had seen more than one-hundred people respond to the invitation to invite Jesus Christ into their lives.

We then went to Brooklyn and conducted a one-week

crusade at a church there. Then we fanned out across the city and saw more young people won to Jesus Christ.

Some of the ministers were antagonistic to this message. Many pastors would even get up in their pulpits on Sunday morning and announce that they wanted none of the young people attending any of the Tom Skinner crusades. They actually warned their people to stay away from them. Of course, that only built up our crowds, because the young people became more curious as to what they were supposed to avoid. They came to hear the Gospel and trust Jesus Christ as their Saviour. And more and more, we saw God successfully winning people to Himself through this very humble ministry that He committed to a group of young people.

In one church, I spoke on a simple gospel story — John 3, where Jesus speaks to Nicodemus about the new birth. I simply told the congregation what it means to be born again into the Kingdom of God, of what it means to have one's spirit remade by Jesus Christ, actually to have Christ come inside and live through you. I gave the invitation for those people who wanted Christ to come into their lives to come forward. Ushers began to leave their posts and walk down the aisle. Robed choir members, seated behind the platform, rose and walked out of the choir. Scores of people across the auditorium, and from the balcony of the church, got up and walked down the aisles.

The minister was seated behind me on the platform. He jumped up out of his seat, almost like a mad-man and ran to the side of the platform where the people of his choir were filing out to come forward. He stopped and loudly said, "What are you going for? You're already in the choir." Then he said to another, "What are you going for? You're president of the choir." He looked down the aisle and saw the president of his usher board coming. He ran off the platform and down the middle aisle of the church. He stopped the president of his usher board and he asked, "What are you going forward for?"

He replied, "Well, he says for all people who want their

sins forgiven to come forward. I want this Christ! I want Him to live in me! I don't know Him!"

One of the deacons got up and came forward. Then another one came forward. And several of the leading officers of his church responded. Like a mad-man, the pastor paced up and down the platform trying to stop the people from coming forward.

Finally, the invitational hymn was over and 125 people stood at the front of the church. The pastor turned to me and said, "What are you going to do?"

I said, "Well, after I pray for these people right here, I'd like to take them downstairs into the basement of your church so I can instruct them on what it means to be a Christian. After they have received Christ, I want to tell them how they can let Christ live through them. I have some literature with me I'd like to give them. I'll show them how they can get a free Bible correspondence course to help them grow and study the Scriptures."

The pastor was frightened. He must have thought, *Boy, with all these people responding maybe this young preacher is going to start a new movement, or a new church. And he will take all my church members away.*

So he said to me, "Look, you know we take the offering for the speaker next." It's customary in some of the Negro churches, after the preacher finished preaching, to take up a "retiring" offering for the preacher. It can be a substantial offering some Sunday mornings — maybe as high as $300.00.

What he was really saying was, "You've got 125 people standing up here! If you take them downstairs and instruct them while we take up the offering for the speaker, these people won't be able to give and your offering will be that much smaller." He thought that by tempting me with money, I would compromise my position and not be able to get to these people. I told him that I would take them down anyway.

He left his assistant pastor in charge and followed me downstairs with the inquirers to be sure that I wasn't telling these people I wanted them to join another church or to join a new movement I was starting. And right in front of him, I asked all those people who had never in their lives received Jesus Christ into their lives to raise their hands. And we counted. There were 125 people altogether down there. Out of 125 people, 117 said they had never received Jesus Christ as Saviour. The other eight were people who had made a profession of faith sometime before, but had drifted away from Jesus Christ. They were seeking reconciliation with God. After I finished instructing these people, and before we returned to the main auditorium where the service was still going on, I asked if there were five people who would be willing to stand up and tell the church why they had come forward.

Two deacons, the president of the choir, one person on the usher board, and one teenager stood up.

The deacon said, "I have been in this church for seventeen years. I have been a deacon in this church seven years. And during all of those years, I have been living a lie. I did not know Jesus Christ. But I thank God that this morning I have come to know Him."

The president of the choir stood up and said, "I've been singing in the choir for years. Many of you have listened to me sing and have told me how much you love the way I sing. But it is only this morning that I can tell you that from now on I will be singing for Jesus Christ."

Each one of them gave a similar testimony. When the service was over, the pastor refused to speak to me.

One Sunday morning I spoke in a church where the pastor had recently died — a chronic alcoholic. As I walked toward the church from the subway that morning, I approached a car with two girls in it. They were embracing, kissing, and making physical love with each other. I tried to ignore them. Lesbianism, homosexuality and illicit sex relations are always taking place in Harlem.

But as I passed the car, they straightened themselves, got out and started walking down the street, holding hands and leaning on each other. They walked into church just ahead of me. I later discovered they both sang in the choir.

Because of the sinful life of the pastor, the church was a den of all kinds of sin. That morning I spoke on a passage from Deuteronomy 1:6, "Ye have dwelt long enough in this mount." And I wasted no words.

"We have been in the mountain of indifference toward Jesus Christ long enough. We have been in the mountain of materialism long enough. We have been in the mountain of immorality long enough." And I stressed the places that we need to move on to, in Jesus Christ.

When I gave the invitation, nearly 300 people came forward. It was a tremendous movement of the Spirit of God. I rejoiced to see all those people coming forward. Never in their lives had these people experienced someone standing up in their pulpit giving a simple invitation for people to invite Jesus Christ to live in them. Not for people to join a church. Not for people to give money, nor to join some movement — just to invite Jesus Christ into their lives. I asked permission to have the inquirers taken downstairs so we could tell them what they were doing and what it meant to come to know Jesus Christ. It disturbed many of the deacons in that church, wondering what I was going to say.

One deacon said to me after the service was over, "You really told the people the truth this morning. You may never get invited to preach back here again, but you at least told the people the truth."

These incidents are typical of hundreds that we encountered in various churches where there was actually hostility toward the Gospel of Jesus Christ. Most of these churches had been conditioned over the years by their pastors and leaders to give the people what they want. "Keep the people happy. Don't say anything that will bother or disturb the people," was usually the philosophy among so many of them. And so, as a result, in many of the Negro churches in America, the people have grown up spiritually starved.

For them, the churches have become a racket. The fantastic part about it is that so many of these churches will know that many of their leaders and many of their pastors are living in open immorality, and will do nothing about it. Often, they will even condone it. It seems they feel that, "If my pastor is immoral, this gives me license to be immoral." In the Negro church in America, there is a crying need for a voice to be raised up, someone to stand and tell the truth about the standards of God.

In so many of these churches, the standard of success among the ministry is based upon how successful or prosperous one is materially or economically. A pastor who is not prospering economically is not considered to be a successful minister. After I preached in a particular church one Sunday morning, the pastor took me into his study and said, "Well, young man, that was a fine message; but if you expect to get any place, I mean, if you really expect to make it, then you can't go on preaching like that. That's *not* what the people want to hear." He walked to the window and pulled aside the drapes to point out his brand new Cadillac in the church parking lot, saying, "The church buys me a new one every year." He opened up a closet in his study, and he showed me some fabulous looking clergy robes that the church bought for him, $500 a piece. He showed me leopard skin capes costing $300.

He said, "You'll never have any of these if you keep preaching that way. And another thing," he added shaking a finger at me, "You're too prudish. If you want to be a successful preacher, you've got to keep the sisters happy. If they want you to go to bed with them, do it — just use discretion. It really gets you a favor when you need it."

I don't know how many times I got "advice" like this. And from clergymen. I'd become depressed, wondering if we could ever make any headway in the battle against Satan *in churches* professing to serve and follow Jesus Christ.

While attending a national convention one year, I was approached by a minister who said, "Are you Tom Skinner from New York?"

I said, "Yes."

"Well, we're planning a party tonight and you're invited; in fact, we've already picked out a girl for you."

I said, "Perhaps you have the wrong 'Skinner' — you're not talking to me."

"Oh yes I am. I heard that you were the prudish type. I heard you were the kind who won't play ball. But listen, man, if you're going to make it, you'd better get with it."

I said angrily, "Listen! God has called me into the ministry. God is the one who is going to bless my ministry. God is the one who's going to take it where He wants it to go. I don't need to 'play ball' with anybody in order to get there."

It breaks my heart to realize that so many of the Negro churches across America have this kind of a "ministry."

13

The Harlem Evangelistic Association

Like oases in a desert, there are earnest, sound evangelical churches in Harlem, really doing an effective job in trying to reach the community for Jesus Christ. One such church is a little one called Emmanuel Chapel.

When I first came into contact with this church, it did not have a pastor. I was invited to speak for several Sundays. One of the members of the church was a young woman by the name of Louise Whittingham, who worked for the Board of Education on Livingston Street in Brooklyn. I had spoken at Emmanuel Chapel several times, and shared the vision together of reaching Harlem for Jesus Christ with her. One evening she called me and told me of her brother, Walter Whittingham, and a couple of other men who were concerned about reaching Harlem for Jesus Christ, men who shared the same vision I did.

On the last Sunday in October, 1961, we met at Emmanuel Chapel. It was Reformation Sunday, the same Sunday Martin Luther a few hundred years earlier had nailed his 95 Theses to the door of the church, starting the Protestant Reformation. Emmanuel Chapel was located on 126th Street and Third Avenue, one floor above a bar. Attending that meeting were Mr. Walter Whittingham, a businessman from Nyack, New York; Mr. George Perry, then the assistant minister of the Soul Saving Station in Harlem; Mr. Jim Ransom, a member of Emmanuel Chapel; Mr. Leonard Perry, a student at Kings College, Briarcliff Manor, New York; Mr. Rupert Bingham, superintendent of the Sunday school at Bethany Missionary Alliance Church; Mr. Larry Thomas, a member of the same church; Mr. John O'Neil, pastor of a church in Long Island; Mr. Donald Carpenter, from East Orange, New Jersey; Mr. Kenneth Thompson, a member of the New York City Police Force; Mr. Dick Braithwaite, a school teacher with the New York City Board of Education, and myself. These twelve men sat down to discuss a vision and burden that each one of us had, to reach Harlem for Jesus Christ. We decided in that meeting to form an evangelistic organization which would be known as the Harlem Evangelistic Association. We laid strategy for an all-out crusade which would be held at the Apollo Theatre in New York City.

These were bold steps to take because none of us had any money. We were not men of notable wealth or material prosperity — just men who were concerned about evangelizing our people in Harlem.

The Apollo Theatre is the center of entertainment in Harlem. It is the place where outstanding Negro performers have started and become famous — Nat "King" Cole, Billy Epstein, Ella Fitzgerald, Duke Ellington, and many other great people started performing years ago at the Apollo Theatre.

The Apollo Theatre used to be the showcase of entertainment for Negroes on the Eastern seaboard. We decided that it would be the place where the Gospel of Jesus Christ would be preached every night for one week during the summer of 1962.

After much prayer, the group decided that I would be the evangelist. We approached the manager of the theatre about the possibility of renting the theatre the following summer. He told us it would cost $5,000.00. It was usually more, but he was willing to take a cut in order to make it possible for us to use the theatre.

But even $5,000.00 seemed like a fantastic amount. None

of us had that kind of money. We soon realized that the $5,000.00 was just to rent the theatre. Above that figure, we'd have to pay a stage crew, theatre employees, the sound crew, the use of the air conditioning for seven days — not to mention the advertising and building of the front of the theatre, the marquee, and the regular advertising we would have to do through radio spot-announcements, newspapers, loudspeakers and posters. We faced the task of organizing a choir, the training of counselors and personal workers. It seemed an impossible job.

We began by first approaching white evangelical Christians in the New York community whom we knew had experience in these things. We went to get their advice and help. But, to my dismay, we met "cold shoulders" from most of the white evangelical leaders in New York City. Many of them thought we were a bunch of ambitious, fanatical young people, who were taking on more than we could handle. Some of them were gracious enough to say, "We'll pray for you, but we could not see how we can really lend any help."

I then became aware of how so many white evangelicals are willing to say that the Negro community needs Christ and needs the preaching of the Gospel, but when it comes to action, they are not willing to join forces with brave and uncompromising Negro evangelicals who make the Gospel of Christ relevant in such a community.

Of course, then we began to approach Negro evangelical leaders of established reputations in New York City. And again, from many of them, we met polite coldness. They said, "It's a wonderful thing you're doing. We're behind you . . . we'll pray for you . . . but we really can't get involved."

Minor doctrinal disagreements kept Negro evangelicals from joining together in a cooperative venture such as the one we proposed.

But we were still convinced this was God's venture. Our group rented an office and began the tremendous ground-

THE HARLEM EVANGELISTIC ASSOCIATION

work necessary for the July Crusade. In March, we started to train counselors, personal workers and a choir.

We began to compile a mailing list for promoting the crusade. The group urged Christians everywhere to begin praying for our spiritual assault on Harlem in July. Before long, we had trained a 150-voice choir and had more than 200 counselors to do the personal work. We started pre-crusade rallies in various churches across the city, and reminded people to stand with us in prayer for this tremendous venture.

Slowly, it seemed as though Christians were seeing the crusade as reality and were beginning to express their interest.

Preparing for the Harlem Crusade in 1962 was tremendously difficult work. It required setting up an office. It required staff in the office and getting volunteer help to come in to help with the typing and the mailings. The other duties were more complex — signing contracts, scheduling advertising, setting up of pre-crusade rallies, the training of the counselors and preparing the counseling material. Much of this kept me up as late as three o'clock most mornings and then rising at eight o'clock to begin a new day. But, to encourage us, God blessed us — great numbers of people were coming to know Christ during the pre-crusade rallies. Lives were being changed. Christians became excited and enthusiastic about evangelism. Negro Christians had been praying for years for God to raise up people who would unite themselves together to assault the Harlem community with the Gospel of Jesus Christ and saw our efforts as an answer to their prayers.

We sensed the urgency of that crusade, because for the first time in quite awhile, unrest was coming to the surface.

Black nationalist leaders were becoming bolder in their threats of violence. While anticipating God's blessing, we also saw seeds being sown for turmoil and unrest throughout the community.

The first Saturday in June, we began conducting mass evangelistic rallies right on the streets of Harlem. We picked

the most populated areas in the Harlem community to conduct crusades every weekend. We chose 116th Street and
Lenox Avenue where more than 3,500 people live within
an area of a single block.

We chose 153rd Street and Bradhurst Avenue and 129th
Street between Seventh and Eighth Avenues, near large
housing developments.

We took the entire crusade choir, all of our personal
workers and set up a large platform with loudspeakers. A
police permit allowed us to have the entire block blocked off
so that there would be no traffic passing through the street.
Then we had the opportunity to minister the Gospel to literally thousands of people.

On strategic Sundays, we conducted rallies right in front
of the Theresa Hotel, on a corner known as Harlem Square.
Everything that is anything in the Negro community can
be discovered on that street corner.

The Theresa Hotel was made famous when Fidel Castro
first came to the United States and met with Nikita Khrush-
chev in Harlem at the Theresa Hotel. That corner was the
sounding board for Malcolm X's emerging philosophy of
black nationalism mixed with the Black Muslim religion.

It had been the place where many thundering statements
were made calling for black unity, sometimes calling for
violence. But, never on that street corner had the Gospel of
Jesus Christ ever been sounded in a mass effort.

There were some who suggested we should not attempt
to preach the Gospel on that street corner because of the
strong feelings of black nationalism. Many black nationalists considered a person who preached the message of
Christ to be an "Uncle Tom," a compromising type of
Negro who puts up with the status quo and is not willing
to fight for his rights.

Many people felt that bodily injury might result for
anyone who went out to preach what was termed "the
White man's religion."

Christianity, they argued, had been given to the Negro to
keep him in his place, and for this reason, thousands of

Christians were afraid to go to such a street corner to make Jesus Christ known. I knew the implications, and yet I felt that God was deliberately calling me to go right into the middle of the controversy and make Jesus Christ known.

In several of the rallies we held in front of the Theresa Hotel, I deliberately chose controversial subjects to attract the crowds and challenge them with the claims of Jesus Christ in my own life. I knew that by some I would be labeled an "Uncle Tom." But I felt there were enough Negroes in Harlem who knew that while I was interested in social, economic and political progress for the Negro, I was more interested in his spiritual progress.

The first message that I preached in front of the Theresa Hotel was a message entitled "The White Man Did It."

I began the message as follows, "Are you a Negro concerned about the problems of the Negro community? If so, we both have something in common. I was born and raised in Harlem, and I have lived in the Harlem community most of my life. Like most people in this community, I am concerned about the problems we face and the so-called 'Negro revolt.' As a boy, I remember asking many people of my race why it was that there was so much crime, immorality, dope addiction, alcoholism, in the community. In most cases the answers went something like this: 'Son, you won't understand this until you are older, but the white man is responsible.' Thus, I have found that many of our race-minded leaders are blaming the white man for the plight of many Negro communities. I wonder just how far we can go with this accusation. There are more than 60,000 dope addicts in Harlem alone. Do you mean to say that a particular race twisted each addict's arm and forced him to take dope? The Harlem community consumes fifty per cent more liquor than it does food, producing hundreds more drunks in our community each day. Is the white man causing the madness that makes many a Negro man stop at the nearest bar with his week's pay rather than going home to his wife and children? Thousands of illegitimate children are born in the Negro community every year. Is the white man standing over our young people with a gun forcing them into immoral affairs? When decent Negro girls cannot walk the streets of their own community without the fear of being molested, it isn't the white man who brings that fear. When concerned parents pray for the day when they can afford to move their children to another community, it isn't the white man they are running from.

"My work requires me to confront these issues every day. Many times in my office or on the streets, I have run into someone with whom I went to school who is now a dope addict, drunkard, or an unwed mother. When I ask them why, they say, 'I don't know. Something made me do it. I didn't want to, but I couldn't help myself.' And that is exactly it. For the Bible teaches us that *all*, Negro *and* white, are born with a nature that is sinful. This sinful nature makes man live contrary to the laws of God, renders him helpless to help himself. In the Bible David says, 'Behold, I was shapened in iniquity, and in sin did my mother conceive me.' The issue in the Negro community is not 'Black vs. White,' but sin in the human heart. It is not necessarily the slums or the environment that makes our community so bad, but the sin in the hearts of the people who live there. Rather than attack a race of people and blame them for our dilemma, let us attack the sinful nature of man. The Bible says, 'Righteousness exalteth a nation, but sin is a reproach to any people.' Man's nature is the reason for the sad conditions of the world. It means that man's present nature must be done away with and replaced with a new one.

"That is exactly what God has done through His Son, Jesus Christ. The Bible teaches us that Christ carried our sinful nature to the cross with Him — 'He was wounded for our transgressions.' It was for *your* sin that Jesus died on the cross. If you will repent of your sin and confess it before God, the Bible declares that God will give you a new nature which will be the very nature of Jesus Christ Himself. The Bible says, 'Therefore if any man be in Christ, he is a new creature. All things are passed away, behold, all things are become new.' Can you imagine what would happen in this Negro community if everyone of us had the nature of Jesus Christ, the Son of God? Even though others refuse Him, it can still happen in your life. The Bible says, 'For as many as received Him, to them gave he power to become the sons of God, even to them that believe on his name.' You can believe, right where you are, that the death of Jesus Christ provided a way for you to be free from your sinful nature. The moment you believe it, Christ will come into your life. If you will trust Jesus Christ, you will find as I have that all the issues of life are met and solved in Him.

"You ask, 'How can I be sure that all you are saying is true?' There is only one way — test it. Ask Jesus Christ to come into your life. Trust Him without a doubt. When He comes in, you will be a new person. Not because you would feel new, but because God's Word says you will be new. Why not invite Christ into your life right now? And trust Him to make you a new person."

At the close of the message, the choir began to sing the invitation hymn, "Just As I Am." My heart was thrilled to see about twenty-five people step out of the crowd and stand beneath the public platform to confess Jesus Christ as their personal Saviour. Once again, we had proven that the message of Jesus Christ is relevant to men's needs and has proven to be the power of God unto salvation to all who believe.

On the street corners, in the crowds and everywhere people gathered, our counselors and choir members personally talked to men and women about their souls. These needy people listened with tears in their eyes as our personal workers told them how Jesus Christ cared about them.

We told them Christ could change them and eventually change the Harlem community. Whether their problem was social, economic or educational, Christ was the answer. Jesus Christ sympathizes with the cause of civil rights, with the struggle for equality, with every man's desire to have enough food for his family, to be able to live where he wants and can afford. He sympathizes with the Negro's desire to be able to go where he pleases to eat, to get a decent education for his children and provide a future for his family. We pointed out that Christ was not opposed to these things, but that they should be no more important than a man's search for God.

The final stages were being set now for the crusade at the Apollo Theatre. We visited various ministerial conferences and spoke to denominational groups in New York City about helping us.

I told them that every effort was being made to raise the finances, now amounting to more than $15,000.00. We were trying to raise all the finances in advance of the campaign so that we would not have to solicit any funds during the crusade. We were hoping that the least emphasis we could place upon money, the better. We knew there would be accusations of our being involved in rackets or simply out for money. This is the reputation many of the Negro churches have given to the Negro community. Immediately after I finished my presentation to a group of ministers, I was verbally attacked.

One minister got up and said, "I cannot support a crusade like this. With all the churches there are in Harlem, where a campaign like this can be held, these young people have decided to go to the Apollo Theatre where there is all kinds of entertainment and burlesque, with half-naked women and all kinds of bad music." He condemned the crusade to be conducted in the Apollo Theatre because the theatre had a history of having burlesque shows on its stage.

Another minister got up and condemned the fact that we were trying to raise all of the money before the crusade started, rather than *during* the crusade. He was one of the biggest fund-raising ministers in the entire conference and more concerned about money than anything else. I suppose he felt that if we succeeded in raising the money in advance of the crusade, that this would be a condemnation of his money-raising tactics.

The ministers' conference refused to endorse the crusade.

I left there that afternoon somewhat dejected, but at the same time a little happy that perhaps the Lord did not want us to be mixed up with them in the first place.

The manager of the Apollo Theatre informed me some weeks later that a group of ministers came to his office and asked him if it was possible for him, in some way, to back out of his contract with us. They used all kinds of pressure to get him to cancel that Apollo Theatre crusade. I began to realize that many of them were really afraid that Harlem would be spoken to by this crusade. They were disturbed that something fantastic would happen. The more opposition we met from different clergymen, the more positive I became that we were in the will of God. He would continue to work out details and supply the funds.

Crusade choirs are an important part of Tom Skinner Crusades. Here is the Harlem Crusade Choir, under the direction of J. Morgan Hodges with Henry Greenidge at the organ, and Vivian Skinner at the piano. On the platform (front row from left to right): Rev. Roger Caesar, Evangelist Bob Harrison, Aaron Hamlin, Rev. Ralph Greenidge, Rev. Jesse Winley, George Perry, Walter Whittingham, Larry Thomas and Norman Smith.

Standing room only. The Harlem Crusade set an attendance record for the Apollo Theatre.

The Apollo Theatre, where such entertainers as Duke Ellington and Ella Fitzgerald have performed became a focal point in Harlem for the preaching of the Gospel of Jesus Christ.

More than 2200 people responded to the invitation to receive Jesus Christ into their lives during the Harlem Crusade. People representing all ages and all the spectrums — economic and social — in the Harlem community responded.

14

The Apollo Theater Crusade

I wonder how many people really know what it means to sacrifice. Negro Christians sacrificed for the Apollo Theatre crusade. Some emptied their savings accounts. Others took additional mortgages out on their houses. Some sold their cars and donated the proceeds. Still others donated a week's salary to the crusade — a few even gave a month's wages.

Finally, the day came for the crusade.

At one o'clock in the afternoon on July 23, 1962, a group of Negro Christians met at the Apollo Theatre for prayer and God's help.

We scattered throughout the theatre. Many people went to the top balconies, some went down the basement, others stood on the stage. We prayed that when the crusade started some six hours later, the Holy Spirit would be present in every corner, convicting the hearts of people who did not know Christ.

The hours before the crusade ticked by slowly. I recalled the struggle of trying to get it all to work. I remembered the months of opposition by churches and black nationalists. These thoughts, and thoughts of how difficult it had been to raise the finances haunted me during the hours before the opening.

I looked around just before the opening. There was a last minute flurry of activity as the staff made a final effort at rehearsal. We would have superb music. My wife, then Vivian Sutton, would play the piano. The organ was to be played by Henry Greenidge, the son of a Christian Missionary Alliance pastor in the Bronx, who at the time of the writing of this book is graduating from Nyack Missionary College. Additional music was to be supplied by the Seale Sisters, five girls and their mother, who have dedicated their lives to singing the praises of God; Ethel Taylor, a young lady who was saved in one of our pre-crusade rallies just one year earlier and who had a magnificent voice that God would use tremendously in attracting people to the Gospel of Jesus Christ; a 150-voice choir under the direction of Mr. J. Morgan Hodges, was ready; the song leader and master of ceremonies every night was George Perry.

My responsibility was to preach.

The tension began to weigh over us all like a thick cloud as we waited for the crusade to begin. One by one, team members came by and put their hands on my shoulder or gripped my arm, assuring me of their prayers and God's interest.

Then the theatre was opened. Almost at once it filled up. A capacity crowd of more than 1,800 was there.

On schedule, the crusade began, and so did the Holy Spirit of God. I experienced unusual liberty in my preaching and when the invitation was given, people responded. We saw broken hearts and tough, sin-hardened people weeping before God in repentance.

Night after night it was the same. We saw people responding to the claims of Christ. It was also interesting, night after night, to look out in that audience and see some of the same clergymen who had fought us, some of the same people of the churches where pastors had stood up in their pulpits and told the people not to attend the crusade. They were jammed into the theatre with others from the community.

Each night it was packed, with standing room only. As the weekend approached, people had to be turned away, and crowds of people had to stand on the outside and listen over loud-speakers. It was the most tremendous moving of the Holy Spirit I had ever experienced.

It would take the writing of another book to tell you about the 2,200 people who came forward to receive Christ during that week of crusade meetings. Drug addicts found Jesus Christ and broke the drug habit; alcoholics found Christ and were freed from alcoholism; broken homes were put back together; frustrated teenagers found new life in Jesus Christ. Today some of these young people are on the mission field, some are studying for the ministry, some are pastors. They found Christ during that crusade and their lives were transformed by the power of God.

We were told by the managers of the Apollo Theatre that we broke the record for attendance of any single event that had ever been held in their history. And our competition consisted of such people as Duke Ellington, Nat "King" Cole, Ella Fitzgerald, Billy Epstein, Ray Charles, and other great rock and roll, jazz, and blues singers. They had gone in and out of there and had tremendous crowds. But more people came to hear the Gospel of Jesus Christ on a single night, than to hear any of these people. We say, "To God be the glory!"

On the last night of the crusade, we conducted a large-scale rally again in front of the Theresa Hotel before moving into the Apollo Theatre for the last meeting. Once again I was led to challenge men and women with the Gospel of Jesus Christ on controversial issues. My message that evening, in front of the Theresa Hotel, was "A White Man's Religion." You see, I knew that most people in the black nationalist movement had been teaching that Christianity was a white man's religion. I decided to peck away at that issue by presenting the claims of Jesus Christ. My message that night went: "Christianity? Why, that's a white man's religion. I want no part of it!

"Christianity was given to the Black man to keep him in slavery!

"The Bible has been changed and added to by the white man in order to brain-wash the Black man.

101

"These are statements that are being made in practically every Negro community in America. The civil rights issue and the struggle for social equality have become such hot issues that many Negroes can only see life in terms of 'black and white.' Many Negroes in their bitterness are denouncing Christianity and the Bible despite the fact that it has been and will continue to be the Black man's only hope. I am a Negro who has lived in the Negro community all my life. Let's you and I, as Negroes, face the issues head on. In the Bible we read these words, 'Look unto me and be ye saved all the ends of the earth, for I am God and there is none else.' Notice first that God says, 'Look unto me.' It does not say, 'Look unto the white man,' but 'Look unto God.' The Bible teaches us that God has seen fit to manifest Himself through His Son, Jesus Christ. So then, it is Jesus to whom we are to look, not any man, black or white. The word 'look' means to draw all our attention to; it means that our very lives are to be surrendered to God through His Son, Jesus Christ. If God demands that we look to His Son, Jesus Christ, it means that Christianity is not a 'religion' but a Person. It is Jesus. Therefore, those who are attacking Christianity as a 'white man's religion' are all wrong! For God's Word, the Bible, is telling us to look unto Jesus.

"The scriptures teach that salvation for any group of people will come only through Jesus Christ. The Bible declares, 'Neither is there salvation in any other, for there is none other name under heaven, given among men, whereby we must be saved.' Notice again, 'Look unto me all the ends of the earth.' It does not say here, 'Look unto me only if you are White.' The Bible teaches us that Jesus died for the sins of the whole world. The scriptures declare, 'God so loved the world (that includes *you*) that he gave his only begotten Son, that whosoever believeth (that means *you*) should not perish but have everlasting life.' The words 'black man' or 'white man' do not appear anywhere in these verses. Many Negroes are falling into the same error they are denouncing by creating religions tail-

102

ored for black people. This is not what the Bible, God's Word, says. The scriptures teach that every man, regardless of race, is born a sinner and will perish in his sins unless he receives Christ personally into his heart.

"The scripture says, 'To as many (black or white) as receive him (that is, Jesus Christ) to them gave he power to become the sons of God, even to them that believe on his name.' I can hear you say, 'If so many White people are really Christians, how do you account for their prejudice?' I will be the first to admit that there have been occasions when I have been disappointed by some people who labeled themselves as 'Christians,' but still maintained hatred in their hearts. But Jesus is saying, 'Look unto *Me*'. He is asking us to focus our attention on Him, not on the prejudices of others. He is asking us to look to Him, not to the social oppression. He is saying, 'I am God. I am the solution to all the paradoxes of life. I am God, and beside me there is none else.'

"The Bible teaches us that the very purpose of Jesus' coming into the world was to do away with the sin that separates us from God and from man. For as long as there is sin in the human heart, it means that man will be separated from God. And when man is separated from God, he is automatically separated from his fellow man. But, thank God, by the death of Jesus on the cross, He has done away with sin, and by His resurrected life, He has made it possible for each of us to belong to a new race. Not the 'white race' or the 'black race' but a third race of men, known as the sons of God, transformed by the power of God. It can happen to you right this moment if you will confess before God that you are a sinner, and then thank Him for taking away your sin on the cross, invite Him into your life. And you will be a son of God this very moment.

"The Bible declares that, 'If any man be in Christ, he is a new creature.' Ask Christ to come into your heart at this very moment and you will be a new person because God's Word says so."

And again, as I gave the invitation for people who really

wanted to trust Jesus Christ, we were thrilled to see scores of people step out of the crowd and invite Jesus Christ to live in their lives.

After the Harlem crusade, we began to pray and plan for the Brooklyn crusade. The crusade was conducted in the month of December, at the Brevoort Theatre in the heart of Bedford-Stuyvesant which was the scene of riots a couple of years ago.

There in that theatre, night after night, for one full week, we again saw people being confronted with the claims of Jesus Christ and responding. And more and more, many of us became aware of the tremendous ministry that God had committed to us in preaching the Gospel to Negroes.

15

The Call to a Wider Ministry

I made no real plans, nor did I ever expect my ministry to reach beyond Harlem. But God had other plans. In the fall of 1962, a call came that expanded my horizons by several thousand miles and marked the beginning of our overseas crusade ministry.

We had received an invitation from the Guiana Council of Evangelical Churches to come and conduct a two-month crusade in that country, then known as British Guiana.

We were present to see the violence and turmoil that caused a delay in the country gaining full independence. It wasn't until May 26, 1966, that independence came and British Guiana became Guyana.

I took an advance team of six with me in December and flew to Guyana.

What a contrast. We left the cold and winter of New York and were transported to what seemed to us to be another world. As our plane banked for a final landing approach, I looked out the window at the dark Atlantic below. Then I saw the lush green of the tropical jungles and the clean-looking city of Georgetown below.

At the airport terminal, the warm, fragrant sub-tropical air filled our lungs as we walked to the customs counter. I looked outside toward the edge of the city. Georgetown was situated on the coast. Just outside the city, the flat

Standing-room-only crowds jam into the community center at Christiana, Jamaica, to hear the Gospel of Jesus Christ each evening.

This man listens attentively as he is told by one of our counselors how simple it is to trust Jesus Christ as personal Saviour. This young man is among the many men who during the May Pen Crusade responded to the invitation to invite Jesus Christ into their lives.

Mr. E. R. Turner conducts follow-up classes at the close of each evangelistic meeting in Jamaica. Scores of people received Jesus Christ into their lives, receiving instructions as to how to go on living the Christian life now that they believe.

Dr. Freddy King, a medical doctor and also one of the chief supporters and planners of the crusade in Christiana, points the way to Jesus Christ as a gentlemen who received Christ that night looks over the follow-up material he has been given.

Louis Simon, who was won to Jesus Christ in prison during the Tom Skinner Bermuda crusade, became one of the counselors during the Christiana Crusade in Jamaica. He is now attending Jamaica Bible School.

countryside stretched many miles in the distance. The six of us were bright with anticipation, looking forward to the crusade.

Guyana is a country with a little more than half a million people. Half of them are East Indians, 31 per cent are Negroes. The East Indian-Negro conflict is a long-standing problem of the country. Three major religions in Guyana — Christians, Hindus and Moslems — are active.

For the next month, we traveled around the country preaching and making preparations for the crusade. The program of training counselors and choir was also begun.

By now our team had grown to 21 members. Our preaching brought souls to Christ and stirred interest in the crusade.

At last the day for the crusade to begin came. We were at the peak of preparation and anticipation. Everywhere we went we were conscious of Christians praying. And I could see our own team earnestly in prayer during those days of preparation. Now we were ready, with God's help.

It was fantastic to see the response, as each night more than 10,000 people jammed onto the Georgetown parade grounds to hear the Gospel. On the weekends, the crowds would be twice that. And night after night, we would see from one to five hundred people respond to the invitation to accept Jesus Christ into their lives.

Our team conducted meetings in hospitals, prisons, churches, peoples' homes, on radio and by every available means to make Jesus Christ known in that country.

There were several experiences that stand out in my mind. A nineteen-year-old East Indian boy was involved in a killing, and his trial was going on during the time that we conducted the crusade at the parade grounds in Georgetown. One Friday night, during the meetings, he was among several hundred to respond to the invitation to invite Christ into his life.

After telling me about his background, he said, "Regardless of the outcome of my court case, I know now that I have the forgiveness of God."

I challenged his statement. "Are you sure you didn't just come forward tonight hoping God would give you some sort of 'good luck' to make the trial turn out favorably?"

He looked down and didn't speak for a moment. Then he looked up at me and replied firmly, "No, I came because I know that I needed Jesus Christ to live in me — regardless of the outcome."

We both smiled as we knew it was real.

On another evening during the course of my message, it began to rain. We were outdoors with no covering around the park. The Guyannese traditionally dislike rain, and whenever rain comes, they head for cover. There were more than 15,000 people present at the meeting that night, and as the rain fell, the first reaction of the crowd was to try and get away. But I continued to preach without stopping.

A Christian friend had brought a business associate along with him to the crusade that night, and as they stood there in the crowd, his friend turned to him and said, "Why doesn't he stop preaching? Why doesn't he just close the meeting and let the people go home? It's raining!"

The Christian said to his business associate, "Well, you see, he's a soldier and soldiers fight under all conditions."

His business associate thought for a moment, then turned and said, "Listen, If he continues to preach in this rain without stopping, then it means that the Christ he is talking about is real and I'll give my life to Christ tonight."

I continued to preach that night and gave the invitation for all who would receive Christ. Soon the crowd came back and stood without moving for the remainder of the message. Many that night responded, and among them was this young businessman who took Christ into his life.

We had been warned not to go to a small city on the coast called Port Morant for a one-week crusade there. Violence and riots related to Guyana's struggle for independence were at a peak.

We were told that Port Morant was the place where there were many revolutionaries who had no use for the Gospel of Jesus Christ. Some had burned the homes of missionaries, preachers, and evangelists. Some missionaries and preachers who lived in the area were stoned and some were even shot! But somehow we felt the compulsion to go.

The crusade meetings were held at the race course stadium in Port Morant. On the last night as I gave the invitation for those who would like to receive Christ into their lives, I noticed at the very top of the stadium two figures emerged from the very rooftop and began to come down the steps. As they came closer, I noticed that they both had on loud red shirts and were carrying long cases in their hands. They turned out to be rifles.

At the close of the meeting, they gave me this story. "We have been sent by the _____ Party in Guyana (a particularly radical political group). I was assigned to shoot you on the first night. I perched on top of the roof, but somehow I could not pull the trigger! It was very mysterious — it was as if something was holding my finger back. I came back the following night. Again I got you in my sight and tried to shoot you — but it still did not work."

His partner nodded soberly. "And when he reported this to the party, that he had not been able to carry out his supposed execution successfully, they sent me with him. Together, both of us were to do it. We perched ourselves up there for two nights in a row, but could not pull the trigger! Neither of us could do it. Now, we decided that what we have been hearing night after night is for us — this tremendous message about One by the name of Jesus Christ who died for us on the cross."

"Are you quite certain He can forgive us? Can we be forgiven of every sin?"

I told them it was very possible — all they had to do was receive Him into their lives and obtain everlasting life.

Both young men were East Indians and of the Hindu faith. They'd had no use at all for the message of Jesus Christ. But when they committed themselves to Christ that night, He took up residence in their lives. Both of them were excommunicated from their homes. They were banned from the community in which they lived. The following day a funeral service was even held for them, in which they were pronounced dead by the entire Hindu community for having embraced Christ.

These two young men are Christians today and are preaching the Gospel throughout the remote areas of Guyana as living testimony that Jesus Christ *does indeed transform lives.*

I had been deeply challenged with some of the dedicated revolutionary characters I met in British Guyana. I met many young men who had just come back from Cuba; some of them were from Moscow and had been well trained in the intellectual thought processes of communism; others had been well-trained in espionage. I will never forget having lunch with one of the leaders of the Peoples' Youth Organization, an arm of the communist party in that country, consisting of young men about 25 years old. One young man told me that even if they had to kill every priest and minister in that country and burn every church to take it over, they were going to do it. I there reaffirmed my own commitment to Jesus Christ that if a communist could die for the cause of communism, I could die if necessary to bring glory and honor to the name of Jesus Christ.

The Guyana crusade lasted for two months. It was a campaign that took much time and patience and prayer, as night after night we ministered the Gospel to thousands of people at the parade grounds and many more by radio, three times a week.

Throughout the city and country, we saw the flames of revival stirring the churches. I suppose that one of the great benefits of the crusade was the fact that we managed to draw evangelicals of like faiths together. Up until that time, the churches were divided.

We were able to see many factions healed, and many of these men who were once bitter enemies became friends and worked together to proclaim the unsearchable riches of Jesus Christ. But I noticed one important issue as I viewed that mission field — how so many white missionaries from the United States bring their little idiosyncrasies and problems from this country to the foreign fields; how they allow the poor natives who become Christians to become caught up in their own conflicts. I would pray to God that the white missionaries of America, when they leave these shores, would leave behind them their petty denominational conflicts and go to the mission field with an open heart to do the one thing they were called to do — to make Jesus Christ known. While these missionaries were fighting with each other over the petty things of doctrine that really did not matter as far as salvation was concerned, the Communists were taking over the country.

But, thank God, we saw His Holy Spirit work in Christian lives, bringing believers together in love and service for Christ.

The Guyana crusade ended in the middle of February, 1963. The full impact of my schedule finally took effect. I was tired. I had lost more than twenty pounds. The schedule of the crusade in Guyana had been gruesome. I decided to go to Bermuda for a vacation rest and to contemplate the future of my ministry and the direction that God would lead. Since I knew no one in Bermuda, I felt that perhaps it was best to go there. I could go out to the beaches and relax for days at a time without having to worry about anyone inviting me to speak at a church, or a rally, or a meeting (I've always found it impossible to turn down such invitations).

I left Guyana on February 17, stopped off at Antigua, and then arrived in Bermuda on the 19th. I had been given a letter by a missionary, Albert Webster, stationed in Guyana, to deliver to Mr. Bill Patterson who resided in Bermuda. A day after my arrival in Bermuda, I decided to look up Bill Patterson. I found him at home. I gave him the letter that Mr. Webster had given to me and we began to spend much time discussing the crusade just finished in Guyana. He was just as excited as I was over what the Lord had been doing there.

Bill had just recuperated from a very serious operation

in Los Angeles, California. He was scheduled to be in Jamaica at that time, but the doctors warned against it because of the serious condition of his health. He had been in a coma for more than five days a short time before.

Bill introduced me to two people that night in Bermuda. One was Mr. F. S. Ferbert, head schoolmaster of Berkeley Institute in Bermuda. Another was Mr. T. N. Tatum, a science teacher at the same school and one of the elders of the local church in the area. Bill invited me to speak in his place on the following Tuesday night at a little Portugese assembly in Middle Road Paget in Bermuda. I accepted the invitation because it would still give me the opportunity to rest and enjoy my vacation.

The Lord worked tremendously in that meeting. Among those present was a young businessman, Mr. Alan Dowdy, assistant manager of a Piggly-Wiggly Supermarket in Bermuda, owned and operated by Mr. Fernance Perry, also a local Christian businessman. These men met with several other businessmen once a week to discuss the Word of God. This prayer group was one of many study groups on the island. They were started by a United States group called International Christian Leadership and the direct assistance of Richard Halverson and others. Several men had been praying for real spiritual awakening in the island. They had asked for Billy Graham to come, but because the churches would not unite together to have such a campaign, it never came about.

These men contacted me several days later and invited me to come down to the office of the supermarket to meet with them.

There, they discussed with me the possibility of staying in the island a little longer and conducting a campaign. I told them that I would have to pray about it since my plans were to have a vacation.

Two days later, after a great deal of prayer and thinking, I gave them the answer that I felt directed by the Lord to stay. Within two days, they called a press conference with the leading television, radio, and newspapers. We laid before them the plans for an all-out crusade in Bermuda. I shared with them a little bit of my background, my personal testimony of how I had come to know Jesus Christ as Saviour and Lord of my life. Within ten days, plans were completed, a committee formed and publicity sent throughout the island. The crusade became front-page news.

At the beginning, the crusade seemed to have produced some problems and skepticism in the minds of some people. You see, Bermuda, although it is from all appearances a peaceful little island, has 30,000 Negroes and 15,000 whites. But the majority of the wealth and the majority of the political power is in the hands of the white people in the island. For a long time, Negroes could not eat in certain restaurants. If they attended the theatres, they had to sit in the balconies. They were not welcomed to certain tennis courts, golf courses, and other resort areas on their own island. Some of these restrictions had been lifted several years prior to my coming, but there was still underlying friction. Election time was coming up within two months, and because of a change in the voting laws, for the first time more colored people than ever before would be voting. More colored candidates were running for the House of Parliament than ever before.

When the Rose Bank Theatre was chosen for the crusade, immediately there was reaction from some of the white businessmen in town who felt that perhaps as a Negro, I had been brought into town to inflame the colored people.

We had a committee meeting with the mayor of Hamilton and several other leaders who wanted to know what I was going to preach. I outlined for them the fact that I had only one message and that was that all men are born into the world detached from the life of God. As a result, there is produced in man what the Bible calls a "sinful nature." This sinful nature can only be eradicated as men receive Jesus Christ into their lives. He died for them, shed His blood to forgive them, and rose again to live in them.

The men were satisfied that I was not a rabble-rouser. But, on the other hand, we had problems from the colored community. They thought I had been brought in by the white businessmen of Bermuda to help maintain the status quo; that my being backed by white businessmen in town to preach the Gospel was their way of saying, "See, we are not so bad. We love the dear colored people and we are backing this dear colored preacher to prove it!"

Antagonism was being produced on both sides, and I was caught in the middle. But generally speaking, there was fantastic anticipation for the crusade. The newspapers gave it tremendous publicity. The radio stations announced it constantly and I appeared on many programs. I appeared on guest programs throughout the island, in various places. I spoke at businessmen's breakfasts, businessmen's luncheons, and banquets. Tremendous interest was being raised for the crusade.

But still there was skepticism as to whether the crowds would really come. Bermudians tend to be a very sophisticated people and generally whenever there are evangelistic crusades held in the island, there are never more than four or five hundred faithful people who come out to hear what is going on.

The crusade opened on Sunday, March 10, 1963. It was scheduled to begin at 9 p.m., to give all the churches on the island time to conclude evening services and to participate if they so desired.

As we drove to the theatre that night and approached the street where the theatre was located, the man who was driving me gasped to see the crowds of people in the street.

His first reaction was that somebody had failed to get there on time to open up the theatre and let the people in. But it was not that at all. We found the theatre had been *full* since 7:30 p.m., and that these *thousands* of people in the streets were people who were trying to get in but there were no more seats available.

Quickly, we made arrangements with the committee. We would empty the theatre at ten o'clock, after having a one-hour service from 9 to 10, and at 10:15 p.m. start another service for the thousands of people in the island who

Capacity crowds appeared everywhere to hear the Gospel of Jesus Christ in Guyana. Here are hundreds of people jammed into one of the community centers along the Essequebo Coast in Guyana, S. A.

One of the young Christian counselors during the crusade held in Mackenzie, a city in Guyana, S. A., points to the Word of God as he shows another young man how he can find life in Jesus Christ.

A counselor shares the peace that Jesus Christ can bring to a young lady during a crusade in Montclair, New Jersey.

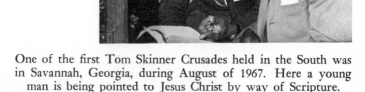

One of the first Tom Skinner Crusades held in the South was in Savannah, Georgia, during August of 1967. Here a young man is being pointed to Jesus Christ by way of Scripture.

Tom Skinner Crusades have exploded the myth that whites cannot operate under Negro evangelical leadership, or that whites cannot communicate effectively to blacks the relevancy of Jesus Christ. In this photograph Mr. Everett Tarver of Augusta, Georgia, shares Jesus Christ with a high school student during the Savannah Crusade.

were not able to attend the first meeting. Quickly, flashes went out on radio and television across the island that those who could not get in the first meeting, could come at 10:15 for the second meeting.

The manager of the theatre had never expected such a fantastic crowd. It was the first time in the history of Bermuda that his theatre had been packed like that for *any* kind of event. With thousands of people milling around outside wanting to get inside the theatre, the manager walked up to Francis Gosling, a merchant in Bermuda, and asked him nervously, "Who is in charge? Who is in charge? Take me to who is in charge!"

Francis was one of the men on the committee for the crusade, and he said to the manager, "Well, the Lord is in charge of this meeting!"

Very disgustedly, the manager threw his hands up in despair and said, "Well then, take me to the number two man!"

As I delivered the message that night, I was aware of unusual power and liberty being given by the Holy Spirit as the message seemed to penetrate every area of the audience. The people sat there attentively listening to the claims of Jesus Christ. The audience was well balanced; in fact, we were told later that it was the first time in the history of Bermuda that such a well-integrated audience had sat together.

Then, the invitation was given for those who wanted Christ to live in them, to come forward. Black and white came together, more than 125 of them, walking down the aisles and standing together. Some were weeping as they asked Christ to forgive them of their sins, and take up residence in them.

The theatre was emptied at ten o'clock while those who responded to the invitation were being counseled backstage. The other people were allowed to enter — and the theatre was again filled with hundreds of people being turned away. Once more, the Gospel was preached and this time more than 150 people responded to the invitation.

Night after night, the scene was the same. We conducted some of the crusade rallies at the Bermuda Athletic Court and invited thousands of teenagers around the island to bring their motorcycles and their transistor radios. As the crusade was being broadcast live from the Athletic field, we asked the teenagers to turn their transistors to the station that was broadcasting the crusade, so that their transistor radios could amplify the field without amplification from a P.A. system. It was a fantastic scene.

Again, scores of people responded to the invitation. And across the island, wherever we went, we saw men and women responding to the claims of Christ; we saw members of Parliament, doctors, lawyers, businessmen saved. People met each other on the buses and talked about how their bosses or fellow employees were being saved. Merchants turned to Jesus Christ and revival was in the air. The Gospel was the talk of Bermuda.

On my final day in Bermuda, I was asked to address the political leaders and the members of the House of Parliament. It was the first time in the history of that country that a minister of the Gospel addressed these political leaders of the island with the claims of Jesus Christ.

I left Bermuda on the 29th of March, 1963, to return to New York City with a tremendous sense of the responsibility that God had called me to make Christ known wherever He took me, to see the message of Jesus Christ become a source of healing between the races and help stem the tremendous racial conflict that exists around the world. The Gospel is the only hope that can stimulate the lives of so many despairing colored people throughout the world who feel oppressed by the white power structure. I knew it could be a source of example to so many whites who desperately need to see that there are men of color in the world who love the Lord Jesus Christ and who are willing to allow Him to live through their lives.

Until these overseas crusades, I had been tremendously burdened for the 22 million Negroes of the United States who so desperately needed to hear the Gospel. Certainly

119

there is enough hopelessness, despair, poverty, and lack of opportunities in America to keep me busy for the rest of my life.

But now I had a *world* vision. Evil, immorality, ignorance and poverty were the daily companions of colored people across the globe. And they, too, needed the Gospel desperately.

I resolved to work even harder, with God's help, in Harlem, across America *and* overseas, as God directed me.

In February of 1964, several of us went as a team from the Harlem Evangelistic Association to the island of Barbados for a three-week crusade. Barbados is a tiny West Indian nation just to the north of the Venezuelan coast. About three-fourths of the people are Negroes. It, too, was experiencing the growing pains of revolution and struggle for independence when we were there.

There again, with crowds averaging five to eight thousand people a night, we presented the claims of Jesus Christ, with more than 430 people responding to the invitation to invite Christ into their lives during the course of the crusade. Again, we became aware of the strong feeling of nationalism that had found its way even into the church. We had been invited to Barbados by the Barbados Council of Evangelical Churches. There was another council in Barbados known as the Barbados Ministerial Council.

The Barbados Ministerial Council claims to be the legitimate evangelical group in Barbados, made up of the white missionaries stationed in the island, as well as some of the leading Barbadian native preachers. The Barbados Evangelical Council consisted mostly of Barbadian preachers who had broken away from the other council on the basis of nationalism. It resented being controlled and dominated by the white missionaries.

We had been invited by the council that had broken away, and as a result, we did not get the complete support and backing of the other churches. Nevertheless, the crusade was successful and people were won to Jesus Christ.

I learned an interesting lesson in Barbados — about being

practical about finances for crusades. Although they provided a house for us to stay in, we had to take care of our own living expenses. Out of our own pockets we had to feed ourselves.

The Harlem Evangelistic Association spent more than $2200.00 in plane fare to get the team down there and back. On top of that expense, we had others. The crusade committee in Barbados gave us $500.00. We were stuck with nearly $2000.00 in expenses. It was then that we began to realize that if we were going to minister the Gospel of Jesus Christ, we had to be very careful about Christians who might take advantage of our desire to reach people for Jesus Christ and not be willing to at least bear our expenses.

I have found much of this in Christian circles even in this country. Churches will invite a preacher to fly across the country to speak at a rally or to conduct evangelistic meetings, and when it is all over, will pat the brother on the back and say, "The Lord bless you." They send him home to his family with a ten dollar bill or a check to cover just his plane fare.

Having been "burned" by the Barbados situation, we have since taken more practical measures to prevent a recurrence of this kind of thing.

A month after our crusade in Barbados, I went alone to the island of Nassau, in the Bahamas, to conduct a three-week crusade.

The crusade was initiated basically through the efforts of Bill Patterson, whom I had met in Bermuda a year earlier. He was now living in Nassau and told the Christians there of the work God had done in Bermuda.

But once again, friction over petty denominational or doctrinal points threatened to derail the plans. One of the participating groups was opposed to my coming, but went along with it because no other speaker could be obtained.

They held back, however, and made plans for a quiet, local campaign instead of the all-out crusade we had planned.

For some of the other Christians in Nassau, it was a matter of racial prejudice. Ninety per cent of the population in Nassau is colored, ten per cent is white. Again, in most cases, the business, financial and political structure of Nassau is controlled by whites. White Christians in some of the local churches in Nassau had aversions to a Negro preacher from America coming to preach to the island. As a result, there was some conflict among some of the believers. Many of them felt that a colored person was not capable of being filled with the Spirit and preaching the Gospel of Jesus Christ effectively to both white and colored people simultaneously.

But on the opening night of the crusade, the hall where the campaign was held was filled to capacity and hundreds of people were out on the streets. They had to put people in another part of the building where loudspeakers allowed them to hear. It was fantastic to see how the Spirit of God worked. And night after night, people stepped out and declared their need for Jesus Christ.

On the weekends, we went to Clifford Park to hold meetings. And again we saw nearly three thousand people come to hear the Gospel.

At the close of the first week, many began to realize that they should have gone all-out. If they had had a bigger campaign and a bigger place, more people would have responded.

I will never forget being present at a communion service in the Central Gospel Chapel on Sunday morning. After the bread was broken, Bill Patterson rose to his feet and spoke to the congregation. He said, "Do you recall the scripture where the disciples came to Jesus Christ saying, 'We have found another one casting out devils and preaching in your Name, but he does not follow us'? And do you remember the reaction of Jesus? In essence, He said that a person who names His name has to be with Him. I draw that parallel because some conflicts have arisen . . . prejudice exists. I challenge us all to confess our sins, to confess the fact that previous to the campaign, we were wrong."

During that day, many went around confessing sin one to

another and seeking forgiveness from God and their Christian fellow-believers. As a result, there was a tremendous breakthrough with more than 265 people responding that night to the invitation. I believe that it confirmed one fact — sin will always block the power of God. Where there is confession of sin and removal of malice from one's heart, there can always be the effective working of the Spirit of God.

This is the only thing that cures the problems of denominationalism, racism, segregation, prejudice, or anything else. When men settle in their hearts the claims of Christ, when there is repentance and people turn their eyes upon Christ, He settles every issue.

During that service, I resolved once more — with God's help — to make my mission world-wide. I prayed God would somehow multiply our seemingly puny efforts.

Yes, thousands upon thousands had heard the Gospel in the past two years and thousands had been saved.

The times would never be more desperate for the Negro to hear the message of Christ and be transformed. If there was a way to increase our ministry in Harlem or overseas, I prayed God would show me.

16

Opportunity Unlimited

I didn't know God would answer my prayer as quickly as he did, and in quite the way that He did.

In August of 1964, we scheduled another Harlem crusade to be conducted at the RKO Regent Theatre in New York City. The crusade dates fell just one week after the Harlem riots of 1964. How I became aware of the urgency of God's message and the desperate need of the community to hear it. We decided to conduct a large-scale rally one Sunday afternoon in front of the Theresa Hotel.

The police allowed us to become the first organization to take to the streets after the ban had been lifted on public meetings. In fact, the Black Nationalist and the Harlem Evangelistic Association had filed simultaneous applications for a mass street rally on that street corner, but the police gave us first preference. That afternoon, in front of the Theresa Hotel, we got complete cooperation. The new Negro captain, who had just been appointed to the precinct, gave us men to maintain order. The police were even willing to donate their loudspeakers. They barricaded travel one way on Seventh Avenue for one-square block so that we could attract crowds. CBS Television covered the entire rally, and much of the message I delivered on that street corner was picked up and televised nationwide on news telecasts of CBS stations across the country. The

New York Times made it a front-page story and gave long excerpts of the message in which we presented Jesus Christ as the only hope for the community.

Afterwards I reflected over the events of the day. Nearly three dozen people were converted for which I praised God — but Jesus Christ was making the front page of the *New York Times* and network radio and television.

Could this be the answer to my prayer? I thought about it, and concluded it was just the beginning. Perhaps we could reach the vast Negro populations of New York and other cities by radio!

I shared this vision with the other fellows on the team of the Harlem Evangelistic Association. Most of them shared my burden and vision, but felt that the organization was not in a financial position to undertake a radio ministry at that time. But somehow I felt the burden that it had to be done, so out of my own pocket I began to undertake a radio ministry. We started on Radio Station WFME, an FM radio station at that time operated by Family Stations of San Francisco.

Within a month, we started on another radio station, WAAA, in Winston-Salem, North Carolina. The city has a population which is 52 per cent Negro. And more and more, the call to reach my people came. I became more and more burdened as riots broke out in other cities. And I knew that the only answer to these social problems was a direct confrontation involving all people of all races with Jesus Christ. In sharing this tremendous vision with the other members of the team, most of them felt that they were not ready to expand their ministry. Most of them felt that the jobs that they had, the responsibilities of supporting their families, and other obligations would not allow them to leave the New York City area or be available full time for such a ministry. But they did commend God's grace upon my ministry and gave me the go-ahead to wherever God was leading me.

So we created an organization known as *Tom Skinner Radio Crusades, Inc.*, which at that time was primarily concerned with buying commercial radio time on Negro radio stations across America to preach the Gospel of Jesus Christ. I also conceived a ministry through tape recordings, sound records, LP's, and literature, to confront people with the claims of Jesus Christ on a level they could understand. I became more and more convinced that a Negro who understood the problems, who sympathized with other Negroes, who had grown up with them, who identified himself with them, but who also exalted Jesus Christ, could communicate with them. We set up our offices at 521 Hopkinson Avenue, in Brooklyn, New York, and there began to embark upon this new ministry that God had given us.

In the fall of 1964, I received an invitation to come to the island of Jamaica in the West Indies to conduct a two-month crusade. Jamaica is probably the most industrial and rapidly growing island in the West Indies. Since its independence in the early 1960's, it has grown fantastically. It has a population of almost two million people. Ninety-seven per cent of the population of Jamaica is colored, the rest being made up of East Indian, European, and what is commonly referred to as Jamaican Whites. Jamaica, as far as I am concerned, is perhaps the perfect example of what a country can be like when it lives together in racial harmony. I was deeply impressed with the way Christians work together and the love and devotion the people in the island who really knew Jesus Christ had for each other. You never heard the terms there, "Is he a white man," "Is he a black man," or, "What color skin does he have?" People referred to each other as human beings. And this is the way I believe God ordained it to be.

I arrived in the island of Jamaica at the end of February of 1965, and stayed until the first of May of that year. We saw fantastic blessings during that nine-week period, as more than 1,800 people made professions of faith in Jesus Christ. Numbers of them were baptized into local Bible-believing churches in the area. When I returned there again in 1966, and again in March of 1967, it was thrilling to see the numbers of them who had received Christ in their lives during those crusade days, now mature and growing in Jesus Christ. It would take another book to describe to you the fantastic results that developed out of that crusade. Peoples' lives were changed. I rejoiced at the tremendous blessing it brought to the lives of Christians as they saw God moving in their midst.

Since that time, the demands on the ministry have been tremendous. We have been called upon to share the claims of Jesus Christ on radio, television. Newspapers across the country have written up my encounter with Jesus Christ and how Christ is working in the hearts and lives of people who are responding to Him, particularly in many of the ghetto areas of America — such as the Hough area of Cleveland where we have conducted crusades, the East side of Detroit, the hill district of Pittsburgh, and many other areas where we have seen Negroes respond on a grass-roots level when confronted with the claims of Jesus Christ.

In the past year, I've had the opportunity to speak of the relevancy of Jesus Christ in hundreds of high schools and on college campuses across America. I've discovered there, a hunger in the hearts of people to know reality and truth. They want to experience His relevancy to the social issues. I'm discovering, particularly among young white people that they are no longer holding the racial views that their parents held before them. They are interested in meeting and knowing Negroes. They want to hear from one who has come up out of the depths of depravity, born and raised in a ghetto area, subject to many of the social injustices that Negroes across America have been subject to, but yet one who has found an answer for it all.

Finally, the ministry that God committed us to in bringing the Gospel of Christ to this vast population of Negroes across America became so overwhelming that I began to pray for God to send additional office help, secretarial help, and that there would be other men raised up to help share in this ministry.

In December of 1966, *Tom Skinner Radio Crusades, Inc.*, was amended to become *Tom Skinner Crusades, Inc.* A

Board of Directors was incorporated into our ministry to help plan and pray with us. They helped set policy and outlined plans as to how to perform this work of evangelism effectively under the direction of the Holy Spirit. Members of the Board of Directors were Dr. Harold Garnes, on the staff of Harlem Hospital in New York City; Dr. Robert Montroy, from White Plains, New York; Mr. John Noel, Director of Bethany Day Nursery in Brooklyn; Mr. Mack Turner, from Bloomfield, New Jersey; Mr. Orin Dudley, President of the New York Bible Society and a Wall Street broker; and Mr. Frank Pickell, an account executive with the Walter Bennett Company of Philadelphia, Pennsylvania. Together, these men, under the inspiration of the Holy Spirit, have brought new life and new vitalization to this ministry of evangelism by radio, and through crusades, personal evangelism, and literature. It has also made it possible for us to bring together and pray and fellowship with other Negro evangelicals of like mind in doing this fantastic job of making Christ known in our times — to match the social revolution with a spiritual revolution.

We want a revolution that will transform the hearts of men, the lives of men, and especially to communicate to black people in America that it is possible to be black and to be free. I mean really free. One does not have real freedom because he has political, social or economic independence. But Jesus Christ says, "Ye shall know the truth and the truth shall make you free." And then Jesus says of Himself in John, chapter fourteen, "I am the way, the truth, and the life. . . ." In other words, to know truth is to know Christ. To know Christ, is to be free. Praise God, I know Jesus Christ, the Lord of heaven and earth, and He is living in me. He will never leave me nor forsake me. I have a security that passes human knowledge. I have had the privilege of watching Him meet every need in my life; He will continue to do so because I know the truth — I know Christ, and Christ has set me free. I am a black man. But I am a free man.

The Seale Sisters have made a wide impact in Tom Skinner Crusades held in various places.

Tom Skinner points to the Book that is the basis for his life, philosophy, and preaching — the Holy Bible, God's Word.

Crowd attending crusade held one week after the Harlem riots in 1964.

High School auditorium in Grand Rapids, Michigan, is jam-packed as students and faculty listen attentively to Tom Skinner talk about his background and his personal encounter with Jesus Christ.

On some nights during a Crusade, the response is so overwhelming that one counselor has to counsel several people at one time.

One of the most important phases of a crusade is to develop sharp, young Negro women who know how to effectively communicate to other women the claims of Jesus Christ.

During crusades, special emphasis is placed upon reaching "kids," (these are youngsters under 12 years of age.)

Hundreds of students listen attentively as Tom Skinner presents the claims of Jesus Christ in the midst of the many social problems in America.

On many nights, the response to the invitation to accept Jesus Christ was so overwhelming that the aisles were literally jammed with inquirers.

17

Some Answers
to Frequently Asked Questions

I would like to close these pages by answering some of the most frequently-asked questions of white evangelical Christians in American society about the Negro and what they consider to be a Negro Christian's answer to these questions.

I do so with a sincere hope that it will challenge the white evangelical community in America to its tremendous responsibility and duty to make Christ known to a unique population of people in America, more than 22 million, most of them dying without hearing the relevant message of Jesus Christ.

This job cannot be done unless you have compassion.

You cannot reach people you are not concerned about. You cannot reach people with whom you do not sympathize.

Will *you* help? Will you sympathize with the social conditions as they exist in the Negro communities across America? Will you share in their aspirations to stand on their own two feet, to be an educated people, to take pride in the color of their skin? We have a culture that goes back far beyond the Civil War and slavery. It goes back centuries when black people were controlling dynasties. Unless you can sympathize with all these things, there is no hope in reaching this vast population.

Of course, in order to work together as Christian men — black and white — we need to understand each other. That's why I'm answering these most often asked questions.

QUESTION: *"What do you think of Black Power?"*

ANSWER: Black power in its strictly conservative, moderate context in the Negro community merely means, "To buy and sell black." In most Negro communities, such as Harlem, Bedford-Stuyvesant in New York, the hill district of Pittsburgh, the Watts district of Los Angeles, the South or West sides of Chicago, the majority of the Negroes who have jobs in these communities work in the white community. They collect their paychecks from a white employer. They then bring their paychecks back into the Negro community and spend their money in stores in the Negro community owned and operated by whites.

It is here that I would like to destroy that myth that you hear that no white person can go into the Negro community and come out alive. The majority of the stores in the Negro community are owned and operated by whites who collect the money and take it back out of the Negro community and bank it back in banks owned and operated by whites.

The Black power concept in its moderate context simply says that the Negro should establish his own stores, build his own banks, establish his own supermarkets, restaurants, sporting good stores, and clothing stores. And he should build them as elaborately and as beautifully as the white stores. Then, he should patronize stores that are owned and operated by Negroes — thus keeping economic power in the Negro community.

Now I recognize that there are extremes to the left and right of this concept. There are those who, by the term "Black Power," mean a total, violent overthrow of the white community. But in the moderate context, it means simply to produce economic power in and for the Negro community; to urge Negroes to run for political office; to urge Negroes to vote for Negroes, send Negroes to the Senate, send Negroes to the City Council as Legislators of their own cities. In other words, get Negroes who can represent Negroes in the Houses of law and legislation in the country. That is the basic concept and moderate point of view of the term, "Black Power."

QUESTION: *"Why do all the Negroes riot?"*

ANSWER: All the Negroes do not riot. You see, when you listen to your radio or watch a television report, you get the idea that every Negro in the Negro community is rioting. But you fail to recognize, for instance, that in Harlem, where almost one million Negroes live, less than two-thousand were involved in the riots. Or, if you go to the recent riots in Newark in 1967 where more than 250,000 Negroes lives, less than 3,000 Negroes were involved in the riots. In other words, all Negroes are not rioting. Where you see riots, it is generally the hoodlum element in the Negro community producing them. The thing that amazes me, of course, is that it has only been since 1964 that the Negro has begun to riot on even that small scale. When you think of all the social injustices he has been subject to — lack of qualified educational facilities, relegated to a slum area, denied decent jobs, not given the right to a decent education, looked upon as "scum" and inferior — it surprises me he hasn't rioted before. It's surprising, especially, when you recall how Negroes were lynched, their homes burned, their women raped, and that there is a whole line of injustices and crimes against the Negro in American society. The thing that we ought to praise and thank God for is that it has only been in recent years that we have seen rioting, and even that rioting has been on a small scale. It might have been larger.

History is very clear — the Negro does have a reason to riot. But for the most part he has shown infinite patience in striving for equality.

QUESTION: *"What did you think of the life and death of Dr. Martin Luther King, Jr.?"*

ANSWER: Martin Luther King was perhaps the most sincere and dedicated leader in the Civil Rights movement. He proved by his life, by his conduct, and by his performance, and by his death that he was willing to die for the cause of Civil Rights. He believed in, and had constantly preached, non-violence as the only philosophy by which the Negro can gain his rights. He constantly urged the black militants to "cool it"; his advice to them was that violence in the end was self-defeating, and an annihilistic philosophy that carried the seed of its own doom. He believed it was a philosophy born of the conviction that the Negroes cannot win, because it fails in the long run to be effective. He preached that any method that fails is ultimately an expression of weakness, not of strength. And he further argued that violence does not appeal to the conscience.

Sometimes it disgusted me to hear white evangelical Christians in American society talking about all the riots and disturbances that Martin Luther King created. Martin Luther King never created a riot or disturbance. Where a riot occurred, it occurred where he was peacefully marching into an area and white bigots attacked him. He had never fought back. I do not know too many white Christians in America who could have been jailed 39 times, beaten, stabbed, had their home bombed, their wife and children threatened, mishandled, lied upon, accused maliciously of being a communist, and still come out each time preaching non-violence and telling his followers not to retaliate. If a group of black militant bigots would come out into the white suburbanite community and begin to burn the community down, and riot and loot and steal, and bring bodily harm against white people, I wonder how many white evangelical pastors would stand up in their churches on Sunday morning and tell their people to turn the other cheek, to love those rioters and to love those looters and not to do any harm to them, but to love them for Jesus' sake.

135

There was no doubt that Martin Luther King was committed to a philosophy of love. The charge that Martin Luther King was a communist was never proven, and I will not accept it as a fact until it is proven. I know that there are certain right-wing Christian extremists who are circulating a photograph of Martin Luther King who is allegedly in some sort of communist training center somewhere in Texas. But a photograph of a man anywhere, does not prove anything. There are people who have taken photographs of me ministering to drug addicts — that does not make me a drug addict. I have visited several communist cellgroups located in Harlem, Bedford-Stuyvesant, to sit down and minister the Gospel of Jesus Christ. And I have called on extreme Black Nationalist groups who believe in the violent overthrow of the government, to talk to them about the claims of Jesus Christ. Perhaps some saw me there, and even took pictures of me with those groups. They could, by the pictures, say that I am a communist, or a Black Nationalist, but I am not. In other words, the claim that Martin Luther King was a communist is unfounded in my opinion. And perhaps one of the biggest problems that white conservative Christians face in America is that any movement that overturns the apple-cart, any movement that disturbs and upsets tends to be labeled communist.

King's views on Vietnam, and the fact that he preached that the United States government should get out of Vietnam, did not make him a communist. There are people in the United States Senate who do not believe we ought to be there. One of our leading Senators, J. W. Fulbright, of the Senate Foreign Relations Committee, does not believe we ought to be in Vietnam — does that make him a communist? It is easy to be a name-caller and to label people with whom we disagree, but our name-calling does not make the label true.

I am not sure that Martin Luther King knew Jesus Christ in the evangelical Christian context. One of the few reporters to interview King on his religious thought, was Presbyterian layman Lee Dirks, of the *National Observer*. Dirks found few traces of the hard fundamentalism in which King was reared. King rejected the idea of original sin; that is, he rejected the concept that a person is born separated from God. Martin Luther King accepted the deity of Jesus Christ, and the fact that Jesus Christ was divine, only in the sense that He was one with God in purpose; he believed that Jesus Christ so submitted His will to God's will, that God revealed His divine plan through Jesus Christ; but he did not accept the fact that Jesus Christ was actually God or actually the Son of God, or God manifested in the flesh. Reflecting much of the liberal instruction he received in liberal institutions, he considered the virgin birth a mythological story which tried to explain that Jesus Christ had moral uniqueness, rather than the fact that His birth was a literal fact — that is His virgin birth.

Even though Martin Luther King did not accept the literal Biblical interpretation of Jesus Christ, he did take the teachings of Jesus Christ on love literally. In many of his speeches and sermons, he referred to Biblical allegations to the love of Jesus Christ. Martin Luther King was able to take the fundamental Christian philosophy in which he was reared, combine it with his liberal education, and weave it through the Bible into the Civil Rights movement to such an extent that he made the Civil Rights movement a very religious movement.

But Martin Luther King had one philosophy that I disagreed with, and which I think is the entire downfall of liberalism in American society, and that is that he believed in the innate "good" of all men; he believed that all men were good basically, and that it was just a matter of creating the circumstances and the situation to bring the good out of men. Yet the very bullet that brought him down, was a reaction against that philosophy. So he felt that he could build a program that would take the good in men and bring it out in society — but the riots, the disturbances, the intense bigotry and racism in America, proved that men are not basically good, but rather basically sinful, and that it takes the regeneration from Jesus Christ alone to change society. Only the Christian revolution that Jesus Christ came to create within the hearts of men, holds our firm hope for a new and better future.

At a conference on urban affairs at Princeton University, a speaker emphasized that America may be counted on to solve her most vexing problems because of man's basic rationality and goodness and faith in liberal progress. When an announcement was suddenly made that King had been murdered, the speaker confessed that his argument was now demolished.

Martin Luther King will go down in history as the man who perhaps made the greatest contribution to the Negro cause in American society. He was an American, he was an apostle of non-violence, he was committed to seeing the democratic principles of America work. He missed one important fact, and that is that man must be regenerated, his attitudes must be changed, a revolution must first occur within his heart, before it can occur in society.

My hope is that a new voice will arise in America to replace the dead voice of Martin Luther King; and that is a voice calling for a revolution in the individual, to carry out the revolution that Martin Luther King wanted to see in society.

QUESTION: *"Can a white person communicate the Gospel of Jesus Christ to a Negro?"*

ANSWER: The answer is yes and no. The answer is "no" if the white person who wants to witness of the saving power of Jesus Christ to a Negro, approaches that Negro paternalistically. In other words, the missionary-type white person who comes to the Negro community and says, "Look at me. I've condescended to come down to speak to you inferiors about Jesus Christ and you ought to be happy about it."

Unfortunately, this is the all-too-true picture we get of many whites witnessing to Negroes. Even if white evangelicals do not *consciously* witness, their attitude is one of superiority and is reflected to the observing Negro.

The only way that a white person can communicate Jesus Christ to a Negro is for him to first win that Negro as a friend. Negroes today, in America, have reached the place where, generally speaking, they are very suspicious of white people. Whenever a white person contacts or approaches a Negro, the Negro's first reaction is "What's your racket?" "What are you up to?" "What are you out for?" "You must have some catch, some gimmick, some game."

The thing that the white evangelical Christian in America must do if he wants to reach the Negro with the Gospel of Jesus Christ is to convince the American Negro that he considers him to be a part of American society.

I remember how bitter I used to get before my conversion recalling the fact that the most segregated hour of the week is eleven o'clock on Sunday morning. The Black Nationalists, before I came to Christ, showed me that the most prejudiced group of people in America are in Bible-believing, white evangelical churches. For a long time, these churches made it sound as if the only way you could get to heaven was to be white, Anglo-Saxon, Protestant, middle-class and Republican!

The Negro will never respond to a white person presenting the Gospel unless it is shown that the Negro is a part of the American society; that he is not inferior; that Christ not only died for him, too, but wants him to have the same hopes, goals, aspirations and fulfillments in life. He needs to know that he can have the same social, economic, psychological, spiritual and physical opportunity as his white contemporary.

When a white man approaches the Negro in honest friendship, Christian love and understanding sympathy, there will be good communications and results.

QUESTION: *"What should the Christian church do when the community changes?"*

ANSWER: I think that the evangelical Christian church in America shows its true colors when the neighborhood begins to change from white to Negro. On one hand we say that the Gospel of Jesus Christ is for everyone and that "God so loved the *world*." But as soon as the neighborhood changes, it is amazing how white evangelical churches pack up and run, get out of the neighborhood, and abandon a mission field perhaps more needy than it was before. As a result, in most of our big metropolitan areas, the inner cities are turning into predominantly Negro areas where there is no sound evangelical church preaching the Gospel. They have all packed up and fled to the suburbs.

Another thing that puzzles me about this is why as soon as the neighborhood changes, the same fundamental church which has been condemning liberals will turn around and sell its church property to a liberal Negro church or far-out cult group, perpetuating the work of Satan in the Negro community and blocking the Gospel message. No one can tell me that this is consistent Christianity. If Jesus Christ died for the souls of white men *and* black men, then it is our job to preach the Gospel to these people and stop running as soon as the neighborhood changes.

QUESTION: *"Won't integration lead to intermarriage and mongrelization of the races?"*

ANSWER: Most white evangelical Christians in America have been given the concept by their parents and grandparents that every Negro male is panting after a white female. But the fact is that down through the years, if you will go back into the annals of slavery in this country, you will find that history bears out the fact that on the slave plantation the white slave master in some cases did not sleep with his own wife. He often slept with one of the more attractive female slaves on the plantation.

His older sons were allowed to continue the tradition by the father, who also "shared" his slave women with passing relatives or friends as part of his "Southern hospitality."

Even the wives of white slave owners and the older daughters on the plantation often had what they called "their own men." These were special slaves — usually strong, handsome young Negro men — who went along to "protect" the women when they rode around the plantation or out into the fields. That slave man in some cases was actually that woman's sexual partner.

The slave had *no* freedom and knew that making any kind of advances meant death. When there was a sexual union between whites and blacks, it was the white slave master or mistress who was the aggressor.

The so-called "mongrelization" of the races has already taken place on a larger scale than it ever will with complete integration of society. The slave owner who sired children; the thousands upon thousands of Negro women who have been raped by white men and the intermarriage of these offspring have produced several shades of skin pigment but have not produced children intellectually or physically inferior.

Out of the thousands of interracial marriages in the United States, the majority are from the upper-middle and upper classes. They are people of superior intelligence who know the old myths are just that — myths. They are people who find each other compatible in every way.

In other words, it boils down to this — the majority of

Negroes in America are not interested in marrying a white person. All the Negro is asking is, "Treat me as a human being. Accept me for what I am. Accept or reject me based on my qualifications and not the color of my skin. Allow me to sit in the same classroom with you and learn from the same professor and take the same examination. Then judge me on the basis of what I have done or performed, not on the basis of what I look like. If you want me to work for you, then pay me the wage that everyone else is making for doing that same work. Don't give me a scaled-down salary because of the color of my skin."

Basically what the American Negro is asking for is a fair shake, an equal opportunity to share in the wealth, the political and social life of America. He is not particularly interested in marrying a white person. The majority of the Negroes I know are interested in marrying within their own race because they — like whites — find people of their own race more attractive.

But from a scriptural point of view, the only separation that the Bible teaches is separation between Jew and Gentile in the Old Testament, and believer and unbeliever in the New Testament. The Bible does not speak out for or against racial intermarriage. However, there are several interesting situations in the Bible. One was the case of Moses, a great Israelite leader, who married an Ethiopian woman. There was no way possible that Ethiopian woman could have been white. She was black because she was Ethiopian. When Moses' sister became angry about it, she got leprosy. How do you explain that? You see, marriages are made in heaven. If two people, born again by the Spirit of God, know Jesus Christ, but happen to have different skin colors, there is no *Biblical* reason for them not to marry. If they both know Jesus Christ and are convinced God brought them together and that it is the will, plan and purpose of God for them to marry, then what I say is, "What God has put together let no man put asunder."

Like the Bible, I do not preach *for* intermarriage or *against* it. I simply say my job is to lead people to Jesus

Christ. After they have received Christ, then it is the responsibility of Christ to be Lord and Master of their lives. If it is God's will for two people to marry — if God has brought them together — it is not my business to try and pull them apart.

QUESTION: *"What are Negro evangelicals doing to try to reach their own people with the Gospel of Jesus Christ?"*

ANSWER: One of the unfortunate situations in the United States is that there are so few Negro evangelicals. Much of this, of course, is due again to the patterns of racial segregation that have existed in this country. Several years ago, when some of our bright young men wanted to go into the ministry and prepare themselves educationally to preach the Gospel, most of the evangelical schools in the United States were closed to them. Those that did open to them, allowed only a certain quota of Negroes. Negroes could not get in the majority of the evangelical schools in America. There are some today who still have in their constitutions and bylaws rules that bar Negroes from being students at their particular Christian college, university or Bible institute. As a result, most of the liberal, neo-Orthodox and radical theological schools opened their doors to Negroes. Consequently, the majority of the Negro preachers in American society today — that is, the majority of the eloquent, fluent, well-educated, well-trained, prepared Negro church leaders — have all been trained in liberal schools because the doors of our evangelical schools were closed to them. This fact stands today to the shame of the prejudiced patterns of the white evangelical world.

And on the other hand, there are Negroes who have dedicated themselves to the work of reaching other Negroes for Jesus Christ. There is the Harlem Evangelistic Association located in Harlem, doing a tremendous job of reaching people on a very limited but effective scale within the Harlem community.

There is also the National Negro Evangelical Association which seeks to bring Negroes of evangelical persuasions across America into a common bond of fellowship and to seek ways and means by which they can effectively communicate the Gospel to their people.

The Gospel Expansion Foundation, with headquarters in Buffalo, New York, seeks to help evangelize the Negro community across America and plant New Testament churches in those areas.

Finally, there is the ministry that God has committed to us, Tom Skinner Crusades, Inc., located in Brooklyn, New York, which has a ministry of radio — to buy radio time on Negro stations across America; to preach the Gospel to the vast population of these people who never hear a sound, relevant message on the air, through mass evangelistic crusades within Negro communities, through Christian literature geared to reach the Negro community. And there is the host of Negro pastors, evangelists, teachers across America who have been effective in reaching the Negro with the Gospel of Christ. Fellows like Bill Pannell of Detroit, Michigan; Bobby Harrison, of California; Howard Jones, with the Billy Graham Evangelistic Association; Ralph Greenwich, pastor of the Bethany Missionary Alliance Church, Bronx, New York City; the late B. M. Nottage, of Detroit, Michigan; T. B. Nottage, of Cleveland, Ohio; Reverend Warren Shelton, pastor of Union Avenue Missionary Alliance Church in Cleveland, Ohio; Walter Whittingham, president of the Harlem Evangelistic Association; George Perry, also of the Harlem Evangelistic Association; William Bentley of Chicago, Illinois; Reverend Ben Johnson, of Christ Baptist Church in Philadelphia; B. Sam Hart, director of the Grand Old Gospel Fellowship of Philadelphia, to name only a few.

The big problem is that many of these churches and evangelistic organizations are in real need of support — prayer support and financial support — to do the effective job of evangelism among their people. You see, evangelism to the Negro is relatively new. We are at least fifty years behind in evangelizing the Negro in this country. Therefore, most Negro evangelical groups cannot depend upon Negroes themselves for much support because Negro evangelicals are so few. *Much of the support must come from the white community.* And if white evangelicals have been willing to spend millions of dollars to convert Negroes in

Africa, we think they would be willing to spend the same amount for Negroes in their own cities. White evangelical Christians must support Negro evangelists and evangelical organizations who are seeking to do an effective work in preaching the Gospel to their people, or the task will never be done.

QUESTION: *"Isn't the Negro basically religious?"*

ANSWER: Again we see a caricature of the Negro instead of the real man. The American Negro is no more or no less religious than the white man. However, the kind of religion usually found in the Negro churches is highly emotional, often superstitious and has little biblical foundation.

I suppose I was typical of most Negro young people. Certainly, I was basically religious — but it was all a front, an act.

Only those — of every race — who have trusted Christ as Saviour and asked Him into their lives, rise above mere religion into a place of absolute faith and commitment.

QUESTION: *"What is your position regarding the race crisis?"*

ANSWER: Basically, it is this: I don't have to go out and struggle for human dignity anymore. Christ has given me true dignity. I don't have to go out and fight for human rights anymore because I have my rights.

You see, I am a son of God. Jesus Christ is living in me and by virtue of the fact that I have received Jesus Christ into my life, the Bible says I have been given the authority to be a son of God. As a son of God, I have all the rights and privileges that go with that rank. I have the dignity that goes with being a member of the royal family of God.

You know, in the world in which we live today, people place great emphasis upon family names, belonging to the right family. While I was at college there were several students who used to spend many hours in the library trying to trace their family tree, to prove that perhaps their great-great-ancestors came across on the Mayflower.

But as a member of the family of God, I am in the best family stock there is. The children of the President of the United States, the Queen of England, or any person who belongs to any socially elite society cannot rank with the position I have as a son of God. And as a member of the family of God, there is not a thing in my life that God is not going to allow me to have, if He wants me to have it.

I know that there will be people who will argue, "Yes. But hasn't the Negro been believing this all of his life? Hasn't the Negro always believed this? And hasn't he continued to be stepped on?" But I am suggesting that basically what has existed in the Negro culture has been nothing more than a religious, culturized kind of Christianity. What the Negro needs in this hour and what the white man needs in this hour is a personal encounter with the Person, Jesus Christ, allowing Christ to live His life through him. Once I have received Jesus Christ into my life, I am no longer a citizen or part of the way of life of a world that is completely contrary to the kingdom of God. I have been translated into a new kingdom and am allowing the head of that kingdom to control and run my life.

And for the first time in my life, my friend, I have *dignity*. For the first time I have a sense of being. I have a sense of being someone. I don't have to struggle for human dignity. I don't have to fight for it. I *am*, present tense, a son of God. I don't have to break my neck to belong to a particular social group to prove it. I don't have to fight to have certain laws passed in order to have me recognized. I have already been recognized by the Lord of heaven and earth as His son.

Secondly, I don't have to go out and fight and struggle for *economic rights*. You see, as a son of God, the Bible tells me that I am an heir of God and a joint heir with Jesus Christ. That means that I have been connected to God to inherit all that God has.

Listen to what God promises. In Philippians 4:19, the Bible says, "My God shall supply all your need according to his riches in glory." In other words, there is not a need in my life since the moment I came to know Jesus Christ that He has not met, isn't meeting right now, and will not continue to meet in the future. Remember, God doesn't lie. I'm reminded of that Scripture where Jesus said to His generation, "If you, being evil, know how to provide good gifts for your children, how much more will your heavenly Father provide for them that love him." In other words, as natural parents we know how to provide for our children. Do you not believe that God — once you've been adopted into His family, once you've received His Son, Jesus Christ — will also provide for *you?*

We're all creatures of God, but we're not all sons of God. The Bible says it is only as many as receive Him, Jesus Christ, that He gave the power to be sons of God.

If it becomes the will of God for me to make $40,000.00 a year as vice-president of General Electric Company, then no power in the world can stop it. And if it becomes the will of God for me to make $350,000.00 a year as president of IBM Company, there is no power in the world that can

150

stop it. In other words, whatever economic status God wants me to maintain on the present earth, as long as I am allowing Him to control my life and run my life, there is no power in all the world that can stop me from being in the place that God wants me to be. Because of Jesus Christ, I am the richest person on the face of the earth.

And thirdly, I do not have to go off and fight for *social status*. Ephesians, chapter four, reminds me that I am seated with Jesus Christ in heavenly places. That puts me on the highest social level in all the world. As a member of the family of God, I am actually seated with Jesus Christ on the highest social level there is in all the world. And I am not about to come down.

In other words, my message to society is very simple. If you want status, maybe you ought to rub shoulders with me because I've got it as a son of God. As a joint heir with Jesus Christ, as a person who is seated together with Jesus Christ in heavenly places, I have everything in this present world that I could ever want.

It doesn't make any difference to me if society doesn't accept me. I have been accepted. It doesn't make any difference to me if society doesn't love me. I am being loved. It doesn't make any difference to me if the rest of society says, "I don't consider you to be my equal." That's their problem. All I know is that Jesus Christ is alive and in me, and because He is living in me, the love of God is actually springing up within my soul. All I ask for is the privilege to love you.

Whether you love me back or not is unimportant. Whether you appreciate the fact that I love you is unimportant. All I ask for is the privilege to love you. I don't ask you to love me back. I make no demands upon you. I don't request that you look upon me as an equal. I don't ask anything of you — just the privilege to love you because of Jesus Christ.

I know that there will be many of my Negro friends who will say that this is nothing but an "Uncle Tom" philosophy, a philosophy that has caused the Negro to be stepped on all these years. I'm going to suggest to you that it's not. I'm going to suggest to you that our white brethren are *in need of real love*. They need an example of love that is found in Jesus Christ. You and I, as Negroes, can point the way to love.

I am convinced that in the midst of this racial crisis in America, we have the privilege through the cross of Jesus Christ to bring this country to its knees in repentance.

When you consider the fact that the Negro in America has paved the way in the music world — in the fields of jazz and rock and roll; he has set the pace in the sports world and the entertainment world — what if he would revolutionize American religious life? What would happen if there were vast numbers of Negro men and women, boys and girls across America who experienced a vital relationship with Jesus Christ? I am convinced that we could lead America back to God. We could lead this pagan, mixed-up, frustrated, so-called culturalized American society to repentance and faith in Jesus Christ. But it can only be done through love.

I'm convinced that hate begets hate, blood begets blood, violence begets violence. Jesus Christ, the innocent Son of God, was subjected to indignity and atrocity heaped upon Him by men whom He had created. I hear Him as He is nailed to a cross, at the peak of injustice, saying, "Forgive them, for they know not what they do."

I've searched my own heart. I've searched my own mind and I've asked myself, "Can I do less? Can I do less than love those who persecute me?" By so shaming them, I would hope that ultimately it would lead them to faith and repentance in Jesus Christ.

I have the deepest respect for the laws, the legislation, and many of the other social action programs that have been instituted to seek to bring America to a place of prominence and respect in the fields of social justice. I have the greatest respect for all of the Civil Rights groups who have dedicated themselves to advance the cause of the Negro in American society. I have the deepest respect for the people who have stepped out on picket lines and who have sincerely demonstrated at the cost of even their lives to make it possible for black men in this country to walk the streets as free men.

But I believe that we must go one step beyond. There's a point where legislation cannot change the human heart. There is a point where social action cannot erase bigotry and hate. There comes a place where a man has to be changed from the inside. His heart has to be dealt with. His feelings, his emotions have to be dealt with. We must remember that prejudice among some people of this country is like a religion and you don't destroy a religion by legislative acts. You don't destroy religion by social action. You don't destroy religion by marches and demonstrations and pickets and wait-ins and sit-ins and pray-ins. If you want to destroy something that is rooted down within the culture of an individual's background, you must deal with him as a person, and again I reiterate, the only Person who can deal with another person is Jesus Christ.

As an individual born on the other side of the tracks; as a kid born in a Negro ghetto; as a kid who grew up with racial hate and bigotry and feelings in his own heart against people who are not of his race, I plead with you to consider the claims of Jesus Christ.

I'm not saying that by receiving Jesus Christ into your life the problem is going to disappear. I'm not saying that by receiving Jesus Christ into your life prejudice is no longer going to exist, that the world is all of a sudden going to be a better place to live; that the bigotry and hatred in our country is suddenly going to be erased. But I am saying simply this — that a commitment to the Person of Jesus Christ will make it possible for you to face these circumstances and overcome them.

There's a tremendous phrase — almost a cliche — which says, "Faith is the victory which overcomes the world." God hasn't promised to remove our circumstances and our problems, but *has* promised a way to cope with them.

I know what it's like to be discriminated against in this

country. I know what it's like to wake up in the morning and look into the mirror and be reminded that you're a Negro, considered by many segments of this society as an inferior. I know what it's like to have the stares and the hate looks. But I also know what it's like to be free. To be a black man, but to be free. To have the color of my skin different, but to have my soul liberated. I know what it is to be a son of God, a joint heir with Jesus Christ, seated together with Jesus Christ in heavenly places, on the highest social level there is in the world. I'm a black man, but I'm a free man.

Tom Skinner autographs copies of his book at the 1968 Winona Youth For Christ International Convention.

TOM SKINNER CRUSADES, INC.
521 Hopkinson Avenue   Brooklyn, New York

*What did you think of
the life and death of
Dr. Martin Luther King, Jr.?*

What do you think of Black Power?

*Can a white person
communicate the Gos-
pel of Jesus Christ
to a Negro?*

*What are Negro evangelicals doing
to try to reach their own people
with the Gospel of Jesus Christ?*

Why do all the Negroes riot?